GW00640796

POCKET COMPANION

2011

ALEKS KRUZ

STEVE WHEELER

FOREWORD BY
JAMES ALLEN

ChequeredFlagMedia

F1
POCKET COMPANION
2011

ChequeredFlagMedia

First Edition Published 2011

Copyright © 2008 - 2011 ChequeredFlagMedia - Aleks Kruz

A CIP catalogue record for this book is available from the British Library

ISBN: 978-0-9565222-1-4

Email: book@ChequeredFlagMedia.com

F1PC2011-S01 (DAKOTA 47)
Printed in the UK by Inprint Litho. www.inprintlitho.com

FOREWORD BY JAMES ALLEN

The 2011 season promises to be another in a series of great years of F1 competition. Since the era of dominance by Michael Schumacher and Ferrari, which ended in 2004, the sport has had a great run of competitive championships with unpredictable outcomes. We have also seen the age of the champions decreasing as first Fernando Alonso, then Lewis Hamilton and Sebastian Vettel lowered the bar.

The competition is intense; in fact since the Schumacher era it has been very hard for anyone to dominate the sport; even with the fastest car it's still easy to make mistakes, both operationally and tactically and that throws the competition open.

I'm particularly excited about 2011 because the combination of new rules and new tyres from Pirelli will make the racing more tactical. We will see the men on the pit wall having to work harder to make the right calls. They will be using their instincts, backed up by lots of quality information. Because to follow this sport properly that is what you need.

In my line of work too, as a journalist and commentator, interpreting the race action and providing in depth analysis of the racing, I rely on intelligence gathering. And being a fan is no different; you need to know what's what, so a pocket companion is a good thing to have about you.

F1 is a complex sport which can be enjoyed on many levels, but to really get close to the action, you need the right information.

I hope you enjoy this book and the 2011 F1 season

JAMES ALLEN

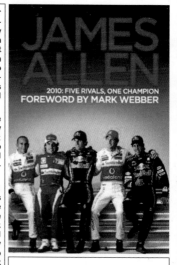

2010: FIVE RIVALS, ONE CHAMPION
FOREWORD BY MARK WEBBER

To Order James Allen's Book

Visit

www.jamesallenonf1.com

Follow on Twitter

www.twitter.com/jamesallenonf1

Live F1 Twitter Feeds

twitter.jamesallenonf1.com

F1

POCKET COMPANION

2011

CONTENTS

ChequeredFlagMedia

FORMULA 1 – 2011 CALENDAR

	LOCATION	CIRCUIT NAME	ROUND / DATE
	AUSTRALIA MELBOURNE	ALBERT PARK GRAND PRIX CIRCUIT AUSTRALIAN GRAND PRIX	1 of 19 25 - 27 March
	MALAYSIA SEPANG	SEPANG INTERNATIONAL CIRCUIT MALAYSIAN GRAND PRIX	2 of 19 8 - 10 April
	CHINA SHANGHAI	SHANGHAI INTERNATIONAL CIRCUIT CHINESE GRAND PRIX	3 of 19 15 - 17 April
	TURKEY ISTANBUL	ISTANBUL PARK TURKISH GRAND PRIX	4 of 19 6 - 8 May
	SPAIN BARCELONA	CIRCUIT DE CATALUNYA SPANISH GRAND PRIX	5 of 19 20 - 22 May
	MONACO MONTE CARLO	CIRCUIT DE MONACO MONACO GRAND PRIX	6 of 19 26, 28 - 29 May
	CANADA MONTRÉAL	CIRCUIT GILLES VILLENEUVE CANADIAN GRAND PRIX	7 of 19 10 - 12 June
	EUROPEAN (SPAIN) VALENCIA	VALENCIA STREET CIRCUIT EUROPEAN GRAND PRIX	8 of 19 24 - 26 June
	GREAT BRITAIN SILVERSTONE	SILVERSTONE CIRCUIT BRITISH GRAND PRIX	9 of 19 8 - 10 July
	GERMANY NÜRBURG	NÜRBURGRING GERMAN GRAND PRIX	10 of 19 22 - 24 July
	HUNGARY BUDAPEST	HUNGARORING HUNGARIAN GRAND PRIX	11 of 19 29 - 31 July
	BELGIUM SPA	CIRCUIT DE SPA-FRANCORCHAMPS BELGIAN GRAND PRIX	12 of 19 26 - 28 August
	ITALY MONZA	AUTODROMO NAZIONALE DI MONZA ITALIAN GRAND PRIX	13 of 19 9 - 11 September
	SINGAPORE (NIGHT RACE)	MARINA BAY STREET CIRCUIT SINGAPORE GRAND PRIX	14 of 19 23 - 25 September
	JAPAN SUZUKA	SUZUKA CIRCUIT JAPANESE GRAND PRIX	15 of 19 7 - 9 October
	KOREA YEONGAM	KOREAN INTERNATIONAL CIRCUIT KOREAN GRAND PRIX	16 of 19 14 - 16 October
	INDIA NEW DELHI	JAYPEE GROUP CIRCUIT INDIAN GRAND PRIX	17 of 19 28 - 30 October
	UNITED ARAB EMIRATES ABU DHABI	YAS MARINA CIRCUIT ABU DHABI GRAND PRIX	18 of 19 11 - 13 November
	BRAZIL INTERLAGOS	AUTÓDROMO JOSÉ CARLOS PACE BRAZILIAN GRAND PRIX	19 of 19 25 - 27 November

Note: Bahrain Grand Prix postponed till further notice. See page 108 for Circuit details.

VODAFONE McLAREN MERCEDES

HISPANIA RACING

MARUSSIA **VIRGIN RACING**

MERCEDES GP PETRONAS
FORMULA ONE™ TEAM

Sauber F1 Team

formula one team

Formula 1
2011

Constructors
2011

Drivers
2011

RED BULL RACING

CONSTRUCTOR PROFILE - 2011

Year Established	2005	Team Principle	Christian Horner
Founder	Dietrich Mateschitz	Phone Number	+44 (0) 1908 279 700
Location	Tilbrook, Milton Keynes	Web Site	www.redbullracing.com
Base Country	United Kingdom	F1 Debut	Australian GP 2005

Formally Stewart (1997 - 1999) • Jaguar Racing (2000 - 2004) • Red Bull Racing (2005 >).

TOTAL STATISTICS - 2005 to 2010			
Grand Prix Involvement	107	Grand Prix Wins	15
Pole Positions	20	Fastest Lap	12
Total Points	754.5	Constructor Titles	1

DRIVER DETAILS - 2011				
Driver	**SEBASTIAN VETTEL - 1**		DEU	www.sebastianvettel.de
Driver	**MARK WEBBER - 2**		AUS	www.markwebber.com
T/R Driver	Daniel Ricciardo		NZL	www.danielricciardo.com
T/R Driver	David Coulthard		GBR	www.davidcoulthard.com
T/R Driver				

Helmets & Car Images Copyright © Red Bull Racing

VEHICLE SPECIFICATION - 2011	
Tyre Supplier: Pirelli Tyre SpA **PIRELLI**	**Chassis:** RB7 **Engine Type:** Renault RS27-2011
	Engine Capacity: 2.4L, V8 90° **RPM:** Limited to 18,000
	www.pirelli.com/tyre/ww/en/motorsport-world

Note: Red Bull Racing 2010 Constructors Champion / Sebastian Vettel 2010 Drivers Champion

RED BULL RACING

TEAM DRIVERS - 2011

SEBASTIAN VETTEL - 1		MARK WEBBER - 2	
Date of Birth	3rd July 1987	**Date of Birth**	27th August 1976
Place of Birth	Happenheim, Germany	**Place of Birth**	Queanbeyan, Australia
Nationality	German	**Nationality**	Australian
Web Site	www.sebastianvettel.de	**Web Site**	www.markwebber.com

DRIVERS STATISTICS

First Grand Prix: USA GP 2007		**First Grand Prix:** Australian GP 2002	
GP Starts: 62	**Wins:** 10	**GP Starts:** 157	**Wins:** 6
Pole Positions: 15	**Fastest Laps:** 6	**Pole Positions:** 6	**Fastest Laps:** 6
Podiums: 19	**Total Points:** 381	**Podiums:** 20	**Total Points:** 411.5
2010 Position: 1st	**2010 Points:** 256	**2010 Position:** 3rd	**2010 Points:** 242

DRIVERS GRAND PRIX HISTORY

2010	**Red Bull-Renault · 256 Pts · 1st WC**	2010	Red Bull-Renault · 242 Pts · 3rd
2009	Red Bull-Renault · 84 Pts · 2nd	2009	Red Bull-Renault · 69.5 Pts · 4th
2008	Toro Rosso-Ferrari · 35 Pts · 8th	2008	Red Bull-Renault · 21 Pts · 11th
2007	Toro Rosso-Ferrari · 6 Pts · 14th	2007	Red Bull-Renault · 10 Pts · 12th
2007	BMW Sauber	2006	Williams-Cosworth · 7 Pts · 14th
		2005	Williams-BMW · 36 Pts · 10th
2006	BMW Sauber · Test Driver	2004	Jaguar-Cosworth · 7 Pts · 13th
		2003	Jaguar-Cosworth · 17 Pts · 10th
		2002	Minardi-Asiatech · 2 Pts · 16th
	Sebastian Vettel		
	Youngest ever F1 World Champion	2001	Benetton-Renault · Test Driver
	(23years 133days)	2000	Benetton-Playlife · Test Driver
	&	2000	Arrows-Supertec · Test Driver
	Youngest ever F1 Driver	1999	Arrows-Arrows V10 · Test Driver
	(19years & 54days)		

Chassis: RB7   **Engine Type:** Renault RS27-2011

SEBASTIAN VETTEL - 1   **MARK WEBBER - 2**

VODAFONE McLAREN MERCEDES

CONSTRUCTOR PROFILE - 2011

Year Established	1963	**Team Principle**	Martin Whitmarsh
Founder	Bruce McLaren	**Phone Number**	+44 (0) 1483 261 000
Location	Woking, Surrey	**Web Site**	www.mclaren.com
Base Country	United Kingdom	**F1 Debut**	Monaco GP 1966

Martin Whitmarsh is currently the chairman of FOTA (Formula One Teams Association)

TOTAL STATISTICS - 1966 to 2010			
Grand Prix Involvement	684	**Grand Prix Wins**	169
Pole Positions	146	**Fastest Lap**	143
Total Points	3835.5	**Constructor Titles**	8

DRIVER DETAILS - 2011				
Driver	**LEWIS HAMILTON - 3**		GBR	www.lewishamilton.com
Driver	**JENSON BUTTON - 4**		GBR	www.jensonbutton.com
T/R Driver	Gary Paffett		GBR	www.garypaffett.com
T/R Driver	Pedro de la Rosa		ESP	www.pedrodelarosa.com
T/R Driver				

Helmets & Car Images Copyright © Vodafone McLaren Mercedes

VEHICLE SPECIFICATION - 2011	
Tyre Supplier: Pirelli Tyre SpA **PIRELLI**	**Chassis:** MP4-26 **Engine Type:** Mercedes-Benz FO 108Y
	Engine Capacity: 2.4L, V8 90° **RPM:** Limited to 18,000
	www.pirelli.com/tyre/ww/en/motorsport-world

Note: MP4 is short for "Marlboro Project 4".

VODAFONE McLAREN MERCEDES

TEAM DRIVERS - 2011

LEWIS HAMILTON - 3		JENSON BUTTON - 4	
Date of Birth	7th January 1985	**Date of Birth**	19th January 1980
Place of Birth	Stevenage, UK	**Place of Birth**	Frome, Somerset, UK
Nationality	British	**Nationality**	British
Web Site	www.lewishamilton.com	**Web Site**	www.jensonbutton.com

DRIVERS STATISTICS

First Grand Prix: Australian GP 2007		First Grand Prix: Australian GP 2000	
GP Starts: 71	**Wins:** 14	**GP Starts:** 189	**Wins:** 9
Pole Positions: 18	**Fastest Laps:** 8	**Pole Positions:** 7	**Fastest Laps:** 3
Podiums: 36	**Total Points:** 496	**Podiums:** 31	**Total Points:** 541
2010 Position: 4th	**2010 Points:** 240	**2010 Position:** 5th	**2010 Points:** 214

DRIVERS GRAND PRIX HISTORY

2010	McLaren-Mercedes · 240 Pts · 4th	2010	McLaren-Mercedes · 214 Pts · 5th
2009	McLaren-Mercedes · 49 Pts · 5th	2009	Brawn-Mercedes · 95 Pts · 1st **WC**
2008	McLaren-Mercedes · 98 Pts · 1st **WC**	2008	Honda · 6 Pts · 15th
2007	McLaren-Mercedes · 109 Pts · 2nd	2007	Honda · 6 Pts · 15th
		2006	Honda · 56 Pts · 6th
		2005	BAR Honda · 37 Pts · 9th
		2004	BAR Honda · 85 Pts · 3rd
		2003	BAR Honda · 17 Pts · 9th
		2002	Renault · 14 Pts · 7th
		2001	Benetton-Renault · 2 Pts · 17th
		2000	Williams-BMW · 12 Pts · 8th
		2000	Williams-BMW · Test Driver
		1999	McLaren-Mercedes · Test Driver
		1999	Prost-Peugeot · Test Driver

VODAFONE McLAREN MERCEDES

Chassis: MP4-26   **Engine Type:** Mercedes-Benz FO 108Y

14

LEWIS HAMILTON - 4   **JENSON BUTTON - 5**

15

SCUDERIA FERRARI MARLBORO

CONSTRUCTOR PROFILE - 2011

Year Established	1929	**Team Principle**	Stefano Domenicali
Founder	Enzo Ferrari	**Phone Number**	+39 (0) 536 949 450
Location	Maranello (MO)	**Web Site**	www.ferrariworld.com
Base Country	Italy	**F1 Debut**	Monaco GP 1950

The meaning of Scuderia, is Italian for "Stable".

TOTAL STATISTICS - 1950 to 2010			
Grand Prix Involvement	812	**Grand Prix Wins**	215
Pole Positions	205	**Fastest Lap**	224
Total Points	4489.5	**Constructor Titles**	16

DRIVER DETAILS - 2011				
Driver	**FERNANDO ALONSO - 5**		ESP	www.fernandoalonso.com
Driver	**FELIPE MASSA - 6**		BRA	www.felipemassa.com
T/R Driver	Giancarlo Fisichella		ITA	www.giancarlofisichella.com
T/R Driver	Marc Gené		ESP	www.marcgene.com
T/R Driver	Jules Bianchi		FRA	www.jules-bianchi.com
T/R Driver				

Helmets & Car Images Copyright © Ferrari SpA

VEHICLE SPECIFICATION - 2011	
Tyres Supplier: Pirelli Tyre SpA	**Chassis:** 150° Italia **Engine Type:** Ferrari 056
PIRELLI	**Engine Capacity:** 2.4L, V8 90° **RPM:** Limited to 18,000
	www.pirelli.com/tyre/ww/en/motorsport-world

Note: The Ferrari 150° Italia is to celebrate the 150 years of Italian unification.

SCUDERIA FERRARI MARLBORO

TEAM DRIVERS - 2011

FERNANDO ALONSO - 5		FELIPE MASSA - 6	
Date of Birth	29th July 1981	**Date of Birth**	25th April 1981
Place of Birth	Oviedo, Spain	**Place of Birth**	São Paulo, Brazil
Nationality	Spanish	**Nationality**	Brazilian
Web Site	www.fernandoalonso.com	**Web Site**	www.felipemassa.com

DRIVERS STATISTICS

First Grand Prix: Australian GP 2001		**First Grand Prix:** Australian GP 2002	
GP Starts: 158	**Wins:** 26	**GP Starts:** 133	**Wins:** 11
Pole Positions: 20	**Fastest Laps:** 18	**Pole Positions:** 15	**Fastest Laps:** 12
Podiums: 63	**Total Points:** 829	**Podiums:** 33	**Total Points:** 464
2010 Position: 2nd	**2010 Points:** 252	**2010 Position:** 6th	**2010 Points:** 144

DRIVERS GRAND PRIX HISTORY

2010	Ferrari · 252 Pts · 2nd	2010	Ferrari · 144 Pts · 6th
2009	Renault · 26 Pts · 9th	2009	Ferrari · 22 Pts · 11th
2008	Renault · 61 Pts · 5th	2008	Ferrari · 97 Pts · 2nd
2007	McLaren-Mercedes · 109 Pts · 3rd	2007	Ferrari · 94 Pts · 4th
2006	Renault · 134 Pts · 1st **WC**	2006	Ferrari · 80 Pts · 3rd
2005	Renault · 133 Pts · 1st **WC**	2005	Sauber-Petronas · 11 Pts · 13th
2004	Renault · 59 Pts · 4th	2004	Sauber-Petronas · 12 Pts · 12th
2003	Renault · 55 Pts · 6th	2002	Sauber-Petronas · 4 Pts · 13th
2001	Minardi-European · 0 Pts · 23rd		
		2003	Ferrari · Test Driver
2002	Renault · Test Driver	2001	Sauber-Petronas · Test Driver
2000	Minardi-European · Test Driver		

WC = World Champion

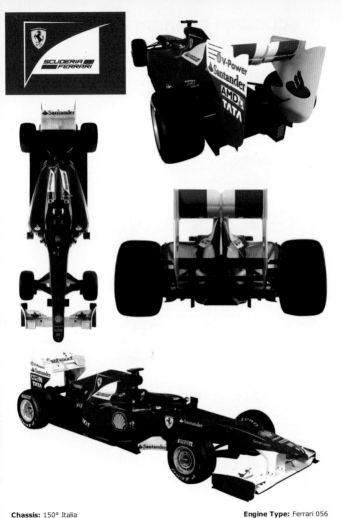

Chassis: 150° Italia

Engine Type: Ferrari 056

FERNANDO ALONSO - 5   **FELIPE MASSA - 6**

MERCEDES GP PETRONAS F1 TEAM

CONSTRUCTOR PROFILE - 2011

Year Established	1954	Team Principle	Ross Brawn OBE
Founder	Mercedes Benz	Phone Number	+44 (0) 1280 844 000
Location	Brackley, Northants	Web Site	www.mercedes-gp.com
Base Country	United Kingdom	F1 Debut	French GP 1954

Formally Tyrrell (1970 - 1998) • BAR (1999 - 2005) • Honda Racing (2006 - 2008) • Brawn GP (2009) • Mercedes GP (2010 >). Mercedes GP acquired Brawn GP in November 2009.

TOTAL STATISTICS - 1954 to 2010

Grand Prix Involvement	31	Grand Prix Wins	9
Pole Positions	8	Fastest Lap	9
Total Points	214	Constructor Titles	0

DRIVER DETAILS - 2011

Driver	MICHAEL SCHUMACHER - 7		DEU	www.michaelschumacher.de
Driver	NICO ROSBERG - 8		DEU	www.nicorosberg.com
T/R Driver				

Helmets & Car Images Copyright © Mercedes-Benz Grand Prix

VEHICLE SPECIFICATION - 2011

Tyres Supplier: Pirelli Tyre SpA	Chassis: MGP W02 Engine Type: Mercedes-Benz FO 108Y
PIRELLI	Engine Capacity: 2.4L, V8 90° RPM: Limited to 18,000
	www.pirelli.com/tyre/ww/en/motorsport-world

    T/R = Test or Reserve Driver

MERCEDES GP PETRONAS F1 TEAM

TEAM DRIVERS - 2011

MICHAEL SCHUMACHER - 7		NICO ROSBERG - 8	
Date of Birth	3rd January 1969	**Date of Birth**	27th June 1985
Place of Birth	Hürth-Hermülheim, Germany	**Place of Birth**	Wiesbaden, Germany
Nationality	German	**Nationality**	German
Web Site	www.michaelschumacher.de	**Web Site**	www.nicorosberg.com

DRIVERS STATISTICS

First Grand Prix: Belgian GP 1991		First Grand Prix: Bahrain GP 2006	
GP Starts: 268	**Wins:** 91	**GP Starts:** 89	**Wins:** 0
Pole Positions: 68	**Fastest Laps:** 76	**Pole Positions:** 0	**Fastest Laps:** 2
Podiums: 154	**Total Points:** 1441	**Podiums:** 5	**Total Points:** 217.5
2010 Position: 9th	**2010 Points:** 72	**2010 Position:** 7th	**2010 Points:** 142

DRIVERS GRAND PRIX HISTORY

2010	Mercedes • 72 Pts • 9th	2010	Mercedes • 142 Pts • 7th
2006	Ferrari • 121 Pts • 2nd	2009	Williams-Toyota • 34.5 Pts • 7th
2005	Ferrari • 62 Pts • 3rd	2008	Williams-Toyota • 17 Pts • 17th
2004	Ferrari • 148 Pts • 1st **WC**	2007	Williams-Toyota • 20 Pts • 9th
2003	Ferrari • 93 Pts • 1st **WC**	2006	Williams-Cosworth • 4 Pts • 17th
2002	Ferrari • 144 Pts • 1st **WC**		
2001	Ferrari • 123 Pts • 1st **WC**	2005	Williams-BMW • Test Driver
2000	Ferrari • 108 Pts • 1st **WC**	2004	Williams-BMW • Test Driver
1999	Ferrari • 44 Pts • 5th	2003	Williams-BMW • Test Driver
1998	Ferrari • 86 Pts • 2nd	2002	Williams-BMW • Test Driver
1997	Ferrari • 78 Pts • DSQ		
1996	Ferrari • 59 Pts • 3rd		
1995	Benetton-Renault • 102 Pts • 1st **WC**		
1994	Benetton-Ford • 92 Pts • 1st **WC**		
1993	Benetton-Ford • 52 Pts • 4th		
1992	Benetton-Ford • 53 Pts • 3rd		
1991	Benetton-Ford • 4 Pts • 14th		
1991	Jordan-Ford • 0 Pts		

WC = World Champion

MERCEDES**GP**PETRONAS
FORMULA ONE™ TEAM

Chassis: MGP W02   **Engine Type:** Mercedes-Benz FO 108Y

  22

| MICHAEL SCHUMACHER - 7 | NICO ROSBERG - 8 |

LOTUS RENAULT GP

CONSTRUCTOR PROFILE - 2011

Year Established	1973	Team Principle	Éric Boullier
Founder	Renault	Phone Number	+44 (0) 1608 678 000
Location	Chipping Norton, Oxford	Web Site	www.lotusrenaultgp.com
Base Country	United Kingdom	F1 Debut	British GP 1977

Renault purchased Benetton in March 2000. Name change from Renault F1 to Lotus Renault GP.
Nick Heidfeld will stand in for Robert Kubica, due to a Rally accident. See page 107.

TOTAL STATISTICS - 1977 to 2010

Grand Prix Involvement	281	Grand Prix Wins	35
Pole Positions	51	Fastest Lap	31
Total Points	1245	Constructor Titles	2

DRIVER DETAILS - 2011

Driver	**NICK HEIDFELD - 9**		DEU	www.nickheidfeld.com
Driver	**VITALY PETROV - 10**		RUS	www.vitalypetrov.ru
T/R Driver	Fairuz Fauzy		MYS	www.fairuzfauzy.com
T/R Driver	Romain Grosjean		CHE	www.romain-grosjean.com
T/R Driver	Bruno Senna		BRA	www.brunosenna.co.uk
T/R Driver	Ho-Pin Tung		CHN	www.hopintung.com
T/R Driver	Jan Charouz		CZE	www.jan-charouz.com

Helmets & Car Images Copyright © Lotus Renault GP

VEHICLE SPECIFICATION - 2011

Tyre Supplier: Pirelli Tyre SpA	Chassis: R31 Engine Type: Renault RS27-2011
PIRELLI	Engine Capacity: 2.4L, V8 90° RPM: Limited to 18,000
	www.pirelli.com/tyre/ww/en/motorsport-world

     T/R = Test or Reserve Driver

LOTUS RENAULT GP

TEAM DRIVERS - 2011

NICK HEIDFELD - 9		VITALY PETROV - 10	
Date of Birth	10th May 1977	**Date of Birth**	8th September 1984
Place of Birth	Mönchengladbach, Germany	**Place of Birth**	Vyborg, Russia
Nationality	German	**Nationality**	Russian
Web Site	www.nickheidfeld.com	**Web Site**	www.vitalypetrov.ru

DRIVERS STATISTICS			
First Grand Prix: Australian GP 2000		**First Grand Prix:** Bahrain GP 2010	
GP Starts: 172	**Wins:** 0	**GP Starts:** 19	**Wins:** 0
Pole Positions: 1	**Fastest Laps:** 2	**Pole Positions:** 0	**Fastest Laps:** 1
Podiums: 12	**Total Points:** 225	**Podiums:** 0	**Total Points:** 27
2010 Position: 18th	**2010 Points:** 6	**2010 Position:** 13th	**2010 Points:** 27

DRIVERS GRAND PRIX HISTORY		
2010	Sauber-Ferrari · 6 Pts · 18th	2010 Renault · 27 Pts · 13th
2009	BMW Sauber · 19 Pts · 13th	
2008	BMW Sauber · 60 Pts · 6th	
2007	BMW Sauber · 61 Pts · 5th	
2006	BMW Sauber · 23 Pts · 9th	
2005	Williams-BMW · 28 Pts · 11th	
2004	Jordan-Ford · 3 Pts · 18th	
2003	Sauber-Petronas · 6 Pts · 14th	
2002	Sauber-Petronas · 7 Pts · 10th	
2001	Sauber-Petronas · 12 Pts · 8th	
2000	Prost-Peugeot · 0 Pts · 20th	
2010	Mercedes · Test Driver	
1999	Prost-Petronas · Test Driver	
1999	McLaren-Mercedes · Test Driver	
1998	McLaren-Mercedes · Test Driver	

DEDICATED TO ROBERT KUBICA

Chassis: R31   **Engine Type:** Renault RS27-2011

NICK HEIDFELD - 9 **VITALY PETROV - 10**

WE ALL WISH YOU A SPEEDY RECOVERY ROBERT
GET WELL SOON

AT&T WILLIAMS

CONSTRUCTOR PROFILE - 2011

Year Established	1967	Team Principle	Sir Frank Williams CBE
Founder	Sir Frank Williams CBE	Phone Number	+44 (0) 1235 777 700
Location	Wantage, Oxfordshire	Web Site	www.attwilliams.com
Base Country	United Kingdom	F1 Debut	Argentine GP 1978

Every Williams F1 car has carried a Senna 'S' somewhere on its livery in honour of Ayrton Senna.

TOTAL STATISTICS - 1978 to 2010

Grand Prix Involvement	539 (565)	Grand Prix Wins	113
Pole Positions	126	Fastest Lap	130
Total Points	2669	Constructor Titles	9

DRIVER DETAILS - 2011

Driver	RUBENS BARRICHELLO - 11		BRA	www.barrichello.com.br
Driver	PASTOR MALDONADO - 12		VEN	www.pastormaldonado.com
T/R Driver	Valtteri Bottas		FIN	www.bottasvaltteri.com/en
T/R Driver				

Helmets & Car Images Copyright © Williams F1. The Senna 'S' Copyright © Instituto Ayrton Senna

VEHICLE SPECIFICATION - 2011

Tyre Supplier: Pirelli Tyre SpA	Chassis: FW33 Engine Type: Cosworth CA2011
PIRELLI	Engine Capacity: 2.4L, V8 90° RPM: Limited to 18,000
	www.pirelli.com/tyre/ww/en/motorsport-world

Note: 565 Points includes 1975 & 1976 as Frank Williams Racing Cars & Walter Wolf Racing.

AT&T WILLIAMS

TEAM DRIVERS - 2011

RUBENS BARRICHELLO - 11		PASTOR MALDONADO - 12	
Date of Birth	23rd May 1972	**Date of Birth**	9th March 1985
Place of Birth	São Paulo, Brazil	**Place of Birth**	Maracay, Venezuela
Nationality	Brazilian	**Nationality**	Venezuelan
Web Site	www.barrichello.com.br	**Web Site**	www.pastormaldonado.com

DRIVERS STATISTICS

First Grand Prix: South Africa GP 1993		**First Grand Prix:** Australian GP 2011	
GP Starts: 304	**Wins:** 11	**GP Starts:** 0	**Wins:** 0
Pole Positions: 14	**Fastest Laps:** 17	**Pole Positions:** 0	**Fastest Laps:** 0
Podiums: 68	**Total Points:** 654	**Podiums:** 0	**Total Points:** 0
2010 Position: 10th	**2010 Points:** 47	**2010 Position:** ———	**2010 Points:** ———

DRIVERS GRAND PRIX HISTORY

2010	William-Cosworth · 47 Points · 10th	**New Driver for 2011**
2009	Brawn-Mercedes · 77 Points · 3rd	
2008	Honda · 11 Points · 14th	
2007	Honda · 0 Points · 20th	
2006	Honda · 30 Points · 7th	
2005	Ferrari · 38 Points · 8th	
2004	Ferrari · 114 Points · 2nd	
2003	Ferrari · 65 Points · 4th	
2002	Ferrari · 77 Points · 2nd	
2001	Ferrari · 56 Points · 3rd	
2000	Ferrari · 62 Points · 4th	
1999	Stewart-Ford · 21 Points · 7th	
1998	Stewart-Ford · 4 Points · 14th	
1997	Stewart-Ford · 6 Points · 14th	
1996	Jordan-Peugeot · 14 Points · 8th	
1995	Jordan-Peugeot · 11 Points · 11th	
1994	Jordan-Hart · 19 Points · 6th	
1993	Jordan-Hart · 2 Points · 17th	

Chassis: FW33   **Engine Type:** Cosworth CA2011

RUBENS BARRICHELLO - 11   **PASTOR MALDONADO - 12**

FORCE INDIA F1 TEAM

CONSTRUCTOR PROFILE - 2011

Year Established	2007	**Team Principle**	Vijay Mallya
Founder	Vijay Mallya/Michiel Mol	**Phone Number**	+44 (0) 1327 850 800
Location	Silverstone, Northants	**Web Site**	www.forceindiaf1.com
Base Country	United Kingdom 🇬🇧	**F1 Debut**	Australian GP 2008

Formally Jordan (1991 - 2005) · Midland F1 / MF1 (2006) · Spyker Cars (2007) · Force India (2008 >).

TOTAL STATISTICS - 2008 to 2010

Grand Prix Involvement	54	**Grand Prix Wins**	0
Pole Positions	1	**Fastest Lap**	1
Total Points	81	**Constructor Titles**	0

DRIVER DETAILS - 2011

Driver	**ADRIAN SUTIL - 14**		DEU	www.adriansutil.com
Driver	**PAUL DI RESTA - 15**		GBR	www.pauldiresta.com
T/R Driver	Nico Hülkenberg		DEU	www.nicohulkenberg.net
T/R Driver				

Helmets & Car Images Copyright © Force India F1 Team

VEHICLE SPECIFICATION - 2011

Tyre Supplier: Pirelli Tyre SpA	**Chassis:** VJM04 **Engine Type:** Mercedes-Benz FO 108Y
	Engine Capacity: 2.4L, V8 90° **RPM:** Limited to 18,000
	www.pirelli.com/tyre/ww/en/motorsport-world

FORCE INDIA F1 TEAM

TEAM DRIVERS - 2011

ADRIAN SUTIL - 14		PAUL DI RESTA - 15	
Date of Birth	11th January 1983	**Date of Birth**	16th April 1986
Place of Birth	Starnberg, Germany	**Place of Birth**	Livingston, Scotland
Nationality	German	**Nationality**	Scottish
Web Site	www.adriansutil.com	**Web Site**	www.pauldiresta.com

DRIVERS STATISTICS

First Grand Prix: Australian GP 2007		First Grand Prix: Australian GP 2011	
GP Starts: 71	**Wins:** 0	**GP Starts:** 0	**Wins:** 0
Pole Positions: 0	**Fastest Laps:** 1	**Pole Positions:** 0	**Fastest Laps:** 0
Podiums: 0	**Total Points:** 53	**Podiums:** 0	**Total Points:** 0
2010 Position: 11th	**2010 Points:** 47	**2010 Position:** — — —	**2010 Points:** — — —

DRIVERS GRAND PRIX HISTORY

2010	Force India-Mercedes · 47 Pts · 11th		**New Driver for 2011**
2009	Force India-Mercedes · 5 Pts · 17th		
2008	Force India-Ferrari · 0 Pts · 20th	2010	Force India-Mercedes · Test Driver
2007	Spyker-Ferrari · 1 Pts · 19th		

Chassis: VJM04

Engine Type: Mercedes-Benz FO 108Y

ADRIAN SUTIL - 14   **PAUL DI RESTA - 15**

SAUBER F1 TEAM

CONSTRUCTOR PROFILE - 2011

Year Established	1993	**Team Principle**	Peter Sauber
Founder	Peter Sauber	**Phone Number**	+41 44 937 90 00
Location	Hinwil	**Web Site**	www.sauberf1team.com
Base Country	Switzerland	**F1 Debut**	South African GP 1993

Formally Sauber Petronas (1993-2005) • BMW Sauber (2006-2009) • Sauber F1 Team (2010 >). Statistics below exclude BMW Sauber era, there were no BMW components used. (2006-2009).

TOTAL STATISTICS - 1993 to 2005 & 2010

Grand Prix Involvement	234 inc 2010	**Grand Prix Wins**	0
Pole Positions	0	**Fastest Lap**	0
Total Points	239 inc 2010	**Constructor Titles**	0

DRIVER DETAILS - 2011

Driver	**KAMUI KOBAYASHI - 16**		JPN	www.kamui-kobayashi.com
Driver	**SERGIO PÉREZ - 17**		MEX	www.sergioperezf1.com/en
T/R Driver	Esteban Gutiérrez		MEX	www.estebangtz.com
T/R Driver				

Helmets & Car Images Copyright © Sauber Motorsport

VEHICLE SPECIFICATION - 2011

Tyre Supplier: Pirelli Tyre SpA	**Chassis:** C30 **Engine Type:** Ferrari 056
PIRELLI	**Engine Capacity:** 2.4L, V8 90° **RPM:** Limited to 18,000
	www.pirelli.com/tyre/ww/en/motorsport-world

Note: BMW Sauber era (2006 to 2009) 70 GP's Involved, 1 Win, 1 Pole Position, 2 Fastest Laps, 17 Podiums, 308 Points. BMW withdrew from Formula 1 motor racing at the end of 2009.

SAUBER F1 TEAM

TEAM DRIVERS - 2011

KAMUI KOBAYASHI - 16			SERGIO PÉREZ - 17		
Date of Birth	13th September 1986		**Date of Birth**	26th January 1990	
Place of Birth	Amagasaki, Hyogo, Japan		**Place of Birth**	Guadalajara, Jalisco, Mexico	
Nationality	Japanese		**Nationality**	Mexican	
Web Site	www.kamui-kobayashi.com		**Web Site**	www.sergioperezf1.com/en	

DRIVERS STATISTICS

First Grand Prix: Brazilian GP 2009		First Grand Prix: Australian GP 2011	
GP Starts: 21	**Wins:** 0	**GP Starts:** 0	**Wins:** 0
Pole Positions: 0	**Fastest Laps:** 0	**Pole Positions:** 0	**Fastest Laps:** 0
Podiums: 0	**Total Points:** 35	**Podiums:** 0	**Total Points:** 0
2010 Position: 12th	**2010 Points:** 32	**2010 Position:** ———	**2010 Points:** ———

DRIVERS GRAND PRIX HISTORY

2010 2009 2008	BMW Sauber-Ferrari · 32 Pts · 12th Toyota · 3 Pts · 18th* Toyota · Test Driver *Stand in for Timo Glock due to accident.	New Driver for 2011

Sauber F1 Team

我々の祈り、
日本に届きますように。

Chassis: C30   **Engine Type:** Ferrari 056

KAMUI KOBAYASHI - 16

SERGIO PÉREZ - 17

SCUDERIA TORO ROSSO

CONSTRUCTOR PROFILE - 2011

Year Established	2005	Team Principle	Franz Tost
Founder	Dietrich Mateschitz	Phone Number	+39 (0) 546 696 111
Location	Faenza (MA)	Web Site	www.tororosso.com
Base Country	Italy	F1 Debut	Bahrain GP 2006

Formally Minardi (1985 - 2005) • Red Bull (2005) • Toro Rosso (2006 >).

TOTAL STATISTICS - 2006 to 2010			
Grand Prix Involvement	89	Grand Prix Wins	1
Pole Positions	1	Fastest Lap	0
Total Points	69	Constructor Titles	0

DRIVER DETAILS - 2011				
Driver	SÉBASTIEN BUEMI - 18		CHE	www.buemi.ch
Driver	JAIME ALGUERSUARI - 19		ESP	www.jalguersuari.com
T/R Driver	Daniel Ricciardo		NZL	www.danielricciardo.com
T/R Driver	David Coulthard		GBR	www.davidcoulthard.com
T/R Driver				

Helmets & Car Images Copyright © Scuderia Toro Rosso

VEHICLE SPECIFICATION - 2011	
Tyre Supplier: Pirelli Tyre SpA	Chassis: STR6 Engine Type: Ferrari 056
PIRELLI	Engine Capacity: 2.4L, V8 90° RPM: Limited to 18,000
	www.pirelli.com/tyre/ww/en/motorsport-world

40   T/R = Test or Reserve Driver

SCUDERIA TORO ROSSO

SÉBASTIEN BUEMI - 18		JAIME ALGUERSUARI - 19	
Date of Birth	31st October 1988	**Date of Birth**	23rd March 1990
Place of Birth	Aigle, Switzerland	**Place of Birth**	Barcelona, Spain
Nationality	Swiss	**Nationality**	Spanish
Web Site	www.buemi.ch	**Web Site**	www.jalguersuari.com/eng/

DRIVERS STATISTICS			
First Grand Prix: Australian GP 2009		**First Grand Prix:** Hungarian GP 2009	
GP Starts: 36	**Wins:** 0	**GP Starts:** 27	**Wins:** 0
Pole Positions: 0	**Fastest Laps:** 0	**Pole Positions:** 0	**Fastest Laps:** 0
Podiums: 0	**Total Points:** 14	**Podiums:** 0	**Total Points:** 5
2010 Position: 16th	**2010 Points:** 8	**2010 Position:** 19th	**2010 Points:** 5

DRIVERS GRAND PRIX HISTORY			
2010	Toro Rosso-Ferrari • 8 Pts • 16th	2010	Toro Rosso-Ferrari • 5 Pts • 19th
2009	Toro Rosso-Ferrari • 6 Pts • 16th	2009	Toro Rosso-Ferrari • 0 Pts • 24th
2008	Toro Rosso-Renault • Test Driver	2009	Toro Rosso-Ferrari • Test Driver
2007	Toro Rosso-Renault • Test Driver	2008	Red Bull-Renault • Test Driver

Chassis: STR6

Engine Type: Ferrari 056

SÉBASTIEN BUEMI - 18   **JAIME ALGUERSUARI - 19**

43

TEAM LOTUS

CONSTRUCTOR PROFILE - 2011

Year Established	2009	**Team Principle**	Tony Fernandes CBE
Founder	1Malaysia F1 Team	**Phone Number**	+44 (0) 1953 851 411
Location	Hingham, Norfolk	**Web Site**	www.teamlotus.co.uk
Base Country	United Kingdom	**F1 Debut**	Bahrain GP 2010

TOTAL STATISTICS - 2010			
Grand Prix Involvement	19	**Grand Prix Wins**	0
Pole Positions	0	**Fastest Lap**	0
Total Points	0	**Constructor Titles**	0

DRIVER DETAILS - 2011				
Driver	**HEIKKI KOVALAINEN - 20**		FIN	www.heikkikovalainen.net
Driver	**JARNO TRULLI - 21**		ITA	www.jarnotrulli.com
T/R Driver	Luiz Razia		BRA	www.luizrazia.com
T/R Driver	Davide Valsecchi		ITA	www.davidevalsecchi.it
T/R Driver	Ricardo Teixeira		ANG	
T/R Driver	Karun Chandhok		IND	www.karunchandhok.com

VEHICLE SPECIFICATION - 2011	
Tyre Supplier: Pirelli Tyre SpA	**Chassis:** T128 (TL11) **Engine Type:** Renault RS27-2011
	Engine Capacity: 2.4L, V8 90° **RPM:** Limited to 18,000
	www.pirelli.com/tyre/ww/en/motorsport-world

TEAM LOTUS

TEAM DRIVERS - 2011

HEIKKI KOVALAINEN - 20		JARNO TRULLI - 21	
Date of Birth	19th October 1981	**Date of Birth**	13th July 1974
Place of Birth	Suomussalmi, Finland	**Place of Birth**	Pescara, Italy
Nationality	Finnish	**Nationality**	Italian
Web Site	www.heikkikovalainen.net	**Web Site**	www.jarnotrulli.com

DRIVERS STATISTICS

First Grand Prix: Australian GP 2007		First Grand Prix: Australian GP 1997	
GP Starts: 70	**Wins:** 1	**GP Starts:** 234	**Wins:** 1
Pole Positions: 1	**Fastest Laps:** 2	**Pole Positions:** 4	**Fastest Laps:** 1
Podiums: 4	**Total Points:** 105	**Podiums:** 11	**Total Points:** 246.5
2010 Position: 20th	**2010 Points:** 0	**2010 Position:** 21st	**2010 Points:** 0

DRIVERS GRAND PRIX HISTORY

2010	Lotus-Cosworth · 0 Pts · 20th	2010	Lotus-Cosworth · 0 Pts · 21st
2009	McLaren-Mercedes · 22 Pts · 12th	2009	Toyota · 32.5 Pts · 8th
2008	McLaren-Mercedes · 53 Pts · 7th	2008	Toyota · 31 Pts · 9th
2007	Renault · 30 Pts · 7th	2007	Toyota · 8 Pts · 13th
		2006	Toyota · 15 Pts · 12th
2006	Renault · Third Driver	2005	Toyota · 43 Pts · 7th
		2004	Renault & Toyota · 46 Pts · 6th
2005	Renault · Test Driver	2003	Renault · 33 Pts · 8th
2004	Renault · Test Driver	2002	Renault · 9 Pts · 8th
2003	Renault · Test Driver	2001	Jordan-Mugen Honda · 12 Pts · 9th
2003	Minardi–Cosworth · Test Driver	2000	Jordan-Mugen Honda · 6 Pts · 10th
		1999	Prost-Peugeot · 7 Pts · 11th
		1998	Prost-Peugeot · 1 Pts · 15th
		1997	Prost-Mugen Honda · 3 Pts · 15th
		1997	Minardi-Hart · 0 Pts · 11th

Chassis: T128 (TL11) **Engine Type:** Renault RS27-2011

HEIKKI KOVALAINEN - 20 **JARNO TRULLI - 21**

HISPANIA RACING F1 TEAM (HRT)

Year Established	2009		Team Principle	Colin Kolles
Founder	Adrián Campus		Phone Number	+34 (0) 96 241 7818
Location	Murcia (Madrid)		Web Site	www.hispaniaf1team.com
Base Country	Spain		F1 Debut	Bahrain GP 2010

Formally known as Campos Meta, also known as Hispania Racing F1 Team and HRT F1 Team.

TOTAL STATISTICS - 2010			
Grand Prix Involvement	19	Grand Prix Wins	0
Pole Positions	0	Fastest Lap	0
Total Points	0	Constructor Titles	0

DRIVER DETAILS - 2011				
Driver	NARAIN KARTHIKEYAN - 22		IND	www.narainracing.com
Driver	VITANTONIO LIUZZI - 23		ITA	www.liuzzi.com
T/R Driver				
T/R Driver				

Helmets & Car Images Copyright © HRT F1 Team

VEHICLE SPECIFICATION - 2011	
Tyre Supplier: Pirelli Tyre SpA **PIRELLI**	**Chassis:** F111 **Engine Type:** Cosworth CA2011
	Engine Capacity: 2.4L, V8 90° **RPM:** Limited to 18,000
	www.pirelli.com/tyre/ww/en/motorsport-world

HISPANIA RACING F1 TEAM (HRT)

TEAM DRIVERS - 2011

NARAIN KARTHIKEYAN - 22		VITANTONIO LIUZZI - 23	
Date of Birth	14th January 1977	**Date of Birth**	6th August 1981
Place of Birth	Coimbatore, India	**Place of Birth**	Locorotondo, Italy
Nationality	Indian	**Nationality**	Italian
Web Site	www.narainracing.com	**Web Site**	www.liuzzi.com

DRIVERS STATISTICS

First Grand Prix: Australian GP 2005		**First Grand Prix:** San Marino GP 2005	
GP Starts: 19	**Wins:** 0	**GP Starts:** 63	**Wins:** 0
Pole Positions: 0	**Fastest Laps:** 0	**Pole Positions:** 0	**Fastest Laps:** 0
Podiums: 0	**Total Points:** 5	**Podiums:** 0	**Total Points:** 0
2010 Position: ---	**2010 Points:** ---	**2010 Position:** 15th	**2010 Points:** 21

DRIVERS GRAND PRIX HISTORY

2005	Jordan-Toyota • 5 Pts • 18th	2010	Force India-Mercedes • 21 Pts • 15th
		2009	Force India-Mercedes • 0 Pts • 22nd
2007	Williams-Toyota • Test Driver	2007	Toro Rosso-Cosworth • 3 Pts • 18th
2006	Williams-Cosworth • Test Driver	2006	Toro Rosso-Cosworth • 1 Pts • 19th
		2005	Red Bull-Cosworth • 1 Pts • 24th
		2008	Force India-Ferrari • Test Driver

WC = World Champion

HISPANIA RACING

Chassis: F111   **Engine Type:** Cosworth CA2011

| NARAIN KARTHIKEYAN - 22 | VITANTONIO LIUZZI - 23 |

51

MARUSSIA VIRGIN RACING

CONSTRUCTOR PROFILE - 2011

Year Established	2009	Team Principle	John Booth
Founder	Manor Grand Prix	Phone Number	+44 (0) 2031 263 929
Location	Dinnington, Yorkshire	Web Site	www.virginracing.com
Base Country	United Kingdom	F1 Debut	Bahrain GP 2010

Formally known as Manor Grand Prix.

TOTAL STATISTICS - 2010

Grand Prix Involvement	19	Grand Prix Wins	0
Pole Positions	0	Fastest Lap	0
Total Points	0	Constructor Titles	0

DRIVER DETAILS - 2011

Driver	TIMO GLOCK - 24		DEU	www.timoglock.de
Driver	JÉRÔME D'AMBROSIO - 25		BEL	www.jeromedambrosio.com
T/R Driver	Sakon Yamamoto		JPN	www.sakon-yamamoto.com
T/R Driver				

Helmets & Car Images Copyright © Marussia Virgin Racing

VEHICLE SPECIFICATION - 2011

Tyre Supplier: Pirelli Tyre SpA	Chassis: MVR-02 Engine Type: Cosworth CA2011
PIRELLI	Engine Capacity: 2.4L, V8 90º RPM: Limited to 18,000
	www.pirelli.com/tyre/ww/en/motorsport-world

Note: Marussia super car manufacturer has a stake in Virgin Racing, hence the team and chassis name change, **www.marussiamotors.ru/en**

MARUSSIA VIRGIN RACING

TEAM DRIVERS - 2011

TIMO GLOCK - 24		JÉRÔME D'AMBROSIO - 25	
Date of Birth	18th March 1982	**Date of Birth**	27th December 1985
Place of Birth	Lindenfels, Germany	**Place of Birth**	Etterbeek, Belgium
Nationality	German	**Nationality**	Belgian
Web Site	www.timoglock.de	**Web Site**	www.jeromedambrosio.com

DRIVERS STATISTICS

First Grand Prix: Canadian GP 2004		**First Grand Prix:** Australian GP 2011	
GP Starts: 54	**Wins:** 0	**GP Starts:** 0	**Wins:** 0
Pole Positions: 0	**Fastest Laps:** 1	**Pole Positions:** 0	**Fastest Laps:** 0
Podiums: 3	**Total Points:** 51	**Podiums:** 0	**Total Points:** 0
2010 Position: 25th	**2010 Points:** 0	**2010 Position:** ———	**2010 Points:** ———

DRIVERS GRAND PRIX HISTORY

2010 Virgin-Cosworth • 0 Pts • 25th 2009 Toyota • 24 Pts • 10th 2008 Toyota • 25 Pts • 10th 2004 Jordan-Ford • 2 Pts • 19th 2007 BMW Sauber • Test Driver 2004 Jordan-Ford • Test Driver	**New Driver for 2011**

WC = World Champion

MARUSSIA **VIRGIN RACING**

Chassis: MVR-02   **Engine Type:** Cosworth CA2011

TIMO GLOCK - 24

JÉRÔME D'AMBROSIO - 25

55

FORMULA 1
2011
GRAND PRIX
CIRCUITS

CIRCUIT
DATA & INFO

CIRCUIT
MAPS & DETAILS

AUSTRALIAN GRAND PRIX - MELBOURNE

Circuit Name : Albert Park Grand Prix Circuit			Round 1 of 19
Number of Laps: **Total Distance:**	58 307.574 km • 191.110 miles	**Lap Record:** **F1 Car:**	Michael Schumacher Ferrari F2004
Circuit Length:	5.303 km • 3.295 miles	**Time • Date:**	1:24.125 • 07/03/2004
Web Site:	www.grandprix.com.au	**Lap Speed:** **(average)**	226.933 km/h 141.016 mph
Address:	Albert Park Grand Prix Circuit, 220 Albert Road, Po Box 577, Melbourne, Victoria 3205, Australia Telephone : +61 3 9258 7100 • Fax : +61 3 9682 0410		

Winners @ Albert Park Grand Prix Circuit

Year • Driver • Constructor	Year • Driver • Constructor
2010 • Jenson Button • McLaren-Mercedes 2009 • Jenson Button • Brawn-Mercedes 2008 • Lewis Hamilton • McLaren-Mercedes 2007 • Kimi Räikkönen • Ferrari 2006 • Fernando Alonso • Renault 2005 • Giancarlo Fisichella • Renault 2004 • Michael Schumacher • Ferrari 2003 • David Coulthard • McLaren-Mercedes 2002 • Michael Schumacher • Ferrari 2001 • Michael Schumacher • Ferrari 2000 • Michael Schumacher • Ferrari 1999 • Eddie Irvine • Ferrari 1998 • Mika Häkkinen • McLaren-Mercedes 1997 • David Coulthard • McLaren-Mercedes 1996 • Damon Hill • Williams-Renault	

Team Winners:	Brawn GP 1 • Ferrari 6 • McLaren 5 • Renault 2 • Williams 1

AUSTRALIAN GRAND PRIX - MELBOURNE

Circuit Name : Albert Park Grand Prix Circuit		25th to 27th March 2011	
Time Zone	GMT +10	**Top Speed**	~325 km/h ~ ~202 mph
Circuit Direction	Clockwise	**Latitude**	37° 50' 59" S
Capacity	118,000±	**Longitude**	144° 58' 6" E
Turns	16	**Years GP Held**	15

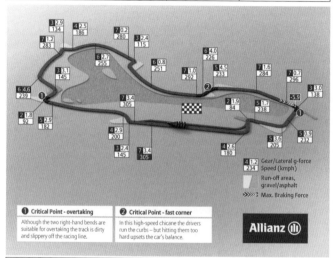

❶ Critical Point - overtaking

Although the two right-hand bends are suitable for overtaking the track is dirty and slippery off the racing line.

❷ Critical Point - fast corner

In this high-speed chicane the drivers run the curbs – but hitting them too hard upsets the car's balance.

Allianz ⑪

2010 Circuit Results : Albert Park Grand Prix Circuit

Position · Driver · Team/Engine · Time/Gap · Speed

Pole Position · Sebastian Vettel · Red Bull-Renault · 1m 23.919s · 227.491 km/h
Fastest Lap · Mark Webber · Red Bull-Renault · 1m 28.358s · 216.061 km/h · On Lap 47

1st · Jenson Button · McLaren-Mercedes · 1h 33m 36.531s · 197.144 km/h
2nd · Robert Kubica · Renault · +12.034s · 196.722 km/h
3rd · Felipe Massa · Ferrari · +14.488s · 196.636 km/h

Notes:

MALAYSIAN GRAND PRIX - SEPANG

Circuit Name : Sepang International Circuit		Round 2 of 19	
Number of Laps: **Total Distance:**	56 310.408 km • 192.887 miles	**Lap Record:** **F1 Car:**	Juan Pablo Montoya Williams-BMW FW26
Circuit Length:	5.543 km • 3.444 miles	**Time • Date:**	1:34.223 • 21/03/2004
Web Site:	www.malaysiangp.com.my	**Lap Speed:** **(average)**	211.772 km/h 131.595 mph
Address:	Sepang International Circuit, Pusat Pentadbiran Litar, Jalan Pekeliling, 64000 KLIA, Selangor Darul Ehsan, Malaysia Telephone : +60 3 8526 2000 • Fax : +60 3 8783 1000		

Winners @ Sepang International Circuit

Year • Driver • Constructor	Year • Driver • Constructor
2010 • Sebastian Vettel • Red Bull-Renault	
2009 • Jenson Button • Brawn-Mercedes	
2008 • Kimi Räikkönen • Ferrari	
2007 • Fernando Alonso • McLaren-Mercedes	
2006 • Giancarlo Fisichella • Renault	
2005 • Fernando Alonso • Renault	
2004 • Michael Schumacher • Ferrari	
2003 • Kimi Räikkönen • McLaren-Mercedes	
2002 • Ralf Schumacher • Williams-BMW	
2001 • Michael Schumacher • Ferrari	
2000 • Michael Schumacher • Ferrari	
1999 • Eddie Irvine • Ferrari	

Team Winners:	Brawn GP 1 • Ferrari 5 • McLaren 2 • Red Bull 1 • Renault 2 • Williams 1

MALAYSIAN GRAND PRIX - SEPANG

Circuit Name : Sepang International Circuit			8th to 10th April 2011
Time Zone	GMT +8	Top Speed	~330 km/h · ~205 mph
Circuit Direction	Clockwise	Latitude	2° 45' 38" N
Capacity	133,000±	Longitude	101° 44' 15" E
Turns	15	Years GP Held	12

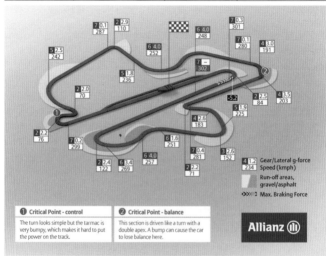

1 Critical Point - control

The turn looks simple but the tarmac is very bumpy, which makes it hard to put the power on the track.

2 Critical Point - balance

This section is driven like a turn with a double apex. A bump can cause the car to lose balance here.

Allianz ⑪

2010 Circuit Results : Sepang International Circuit

Position · Driver · Team/Engine · Time/Gap · Speed

Pole Position · Mark Webber · Red Bull-Renault · 1m 49.327s · 182.524 km/h
Fastest Lap · Mark Webber · Red Bull-Renault · 1m 37.054s · 205.605 km/h · On Lap 53

1st · Sebastian Vettel · Red Bull-Renault · 1h 33m 48.412s · 198.540 km/h
2nd · Mark Webber · Red Bull-Renault · +4.849s · 198.369 km/h
3rd · Nico Rosberg · Mercedes · +13.504s · 198.065 km/h

Notes:

CHINESE GRAND PRIX - SHANGHAI

Circuit Name : Shanghai International Circuit			Round 3 of 19
Number of Laps: **Total Distance:**	56 305.066 km • 189.568 miles	**Lap Record:** **F1 Car:**	Michael Schumacher Ferrari F2004
Circuit Length:	5.451 km • 3.387 miles	**Time • Date:**	1:32.238 • 26/09/2004
Web Site:	www.icsh.sh.cn www.f1china.com.cn	**Lap Speed:** **(average)**	212.749 km/h 132.202 mph
Address:	Shanghai International Circuit, 29/F Jiushi Towers, 28 Zhongshanng Road (South), 200010 Shanghai, China Telephone : +86 21 633 05555 • Fax : +82 21 633 06655		

Winners @ Shanghai International Circuit

Year • Driver • Constructor	Year • Driver • Constructor
2010 • Jenson Button • McLaren-Mercedes 2009 • Sebastian Vettel • Red Bull-Renault 2008 • Lewis Hamilton • McLaren-Mercedes 2007 • Kimi Räikkönen • Ferrari 2006 • Michael Schumacher • Ferrari 2005 • Fernando Alonso • Renault 2004 • Rubens Barrichello • Ferrari	

Team Winners:	Ferrari 3 • McLaren 2 • Red Bull 1 • Renault 1

CHINESE GRAND PRIX - SHANGHAI

Circuit Name : Shanghai International Circuit			15th to 17th April 2011
Time Zone	GMT +8	**Top Speed**	~320 km/h • ~199 mph
Circuit Direction	Clockwise	**Latitude**	31° 20' 20" N
Capacity	200,000±	**Longitude**	121° 13' 11" E
Turns	16	**Years GP Held**	7

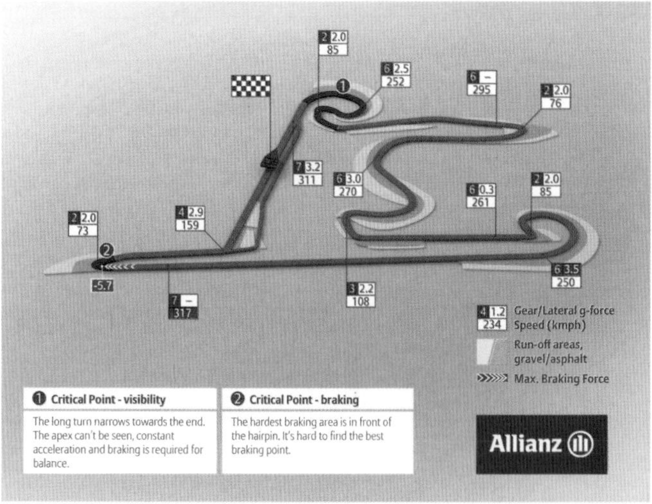
2 2.0 85
6 2.5 252
6 – 295
2 2.0 76
7 3.2 311
6 3.0 270
6 0.3 261
2 2.0 85
2 2.0 73
4 2.9 159
-5.7
7 – 317
3 2.2 108
6 3.5 250
4 1.2 Gear/Lateral g-force
234 Speed (kmph)
Run-off areas, gravel/asphalt
Max. Braking Force
1 Critical Point - visibility
The long turn narrows towards the end. The apex can't be seen, constant acceleration and braking is required for balance.
2 Critical Point - braking
The hardest braking area is in front of the hairpin. It's hard to find the best braking point.
Allianz

2010 Circuit Results : Shanghai International Circuit

Position • Driver • Team/Engine • Time/Gap • Speed

Pole Position • Sebastian Vettel • Red Bull-Renault • 1m 34.558s • 207.530 km/h
Fastest Lap • Lewis Hamilton • McLaren-Mercedes • 1m 46.061s • 192.273 km/h • On Lap 13

1st • Lewis Hamilton • McLaren-Mercedes • 1h 46m 42.163s • 171.541 km/h
2nd • Robert Kubica • Renault • +1.530s • 171.500 km/h
3rd • Felipe Massa • Ferrari • +9.484s • 171.287 km/h

Notes:

TURKISH GRAND PRIX - ISTANBUL

Circuit Name : Istanbul Park			Round 4 of 19
Number of Laps: **Total Distance:**	58 309.396 km · 192.250 miles	**Lap Record:** **F1 Car:**	Juan Pablo Montoya McLaren MP4/20
Circuit Length:	5.338 km · 3.317 miles	**Time · Date:**	1:24.770 · 21/08/2005
Web Site:	www.istanbulparkcircuit.com	**Lap Speed:** **(average)**	222.167 km/h 138.096 mph
Address:	Istanbul Park, Göçbeyli Köyü Yolu 34959 Tuzla, Istanbul, Turkey		
	Telephone : +90 216 677 1010 · Fax : +90 216 677 1039		

Winners @ Istanbul Park

Year · Driver · Constructor	Year · Driver · Constructor
2010 · Lewis Hamilton · McLaren-Mercedes 2009 · Jenson Button · Brawn-Mercedes 2008 · Felipe Massa · Ferrari 2007 · Felipe Massa · Ferrari 2006 · Felipe Massa · Ferrari 2005 · Kimi Räikkönen · McLaren-Mercedes	

Team Winners:	Brawn GP 1 · Ferrari 3 · McLaren 2

TURKISH GRAND PRIX - ISTANBUL

Circuit Name : Istanbul Park			6th to 8th May 2011
Time Zone	GMT +2	Top Speed	~320 km/h • ~199 mph
Circuit Direction	Anticlockwise	Latitude	40° 57' 6" N
Capacity	160,000±	Longitude	29° 24' 18" E
Turns	14	Years GP Held	6

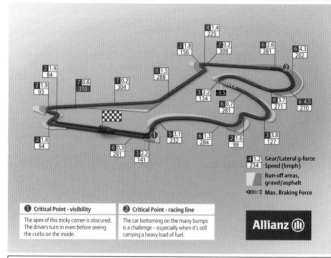

❶ Critical Point - visibility

The apex of this tricky corner is obscured. The drivers turn in even before seeing the curbs on the inside.

❷ Critical Point - racing line

The car bottoming on the many bumps is a challenge – especially when it's still carrying a heavy load of fuel.

Gear/Lateral g-force
Speed (kmph)
Run-off areas, gravel/asphalt
Max. Braking Force

Allianz ⑪

2010 Circuit Results : Istanbul Park

Position • Driver • Team/Engine • Time/Gap • Speed

Pole Position • Mark Webber • Red Bull-Renault • 1m 26.295s • 222.687 km/h
Fastest Lap • Vitaly Petrov • Renault • 1m 29.165s • 215.519 km/h • On Lap 57

1st • Lewis Hamilton • McLaren-Mercedes • 1h 28m 47.620s • 209.066 km/h
2nd • Jenson Button • McLaren-Mercedes • +2.645s • 208.962 km/h
3rd • Mark Webber • Red Bull-Renault • +24.285s • 208.117 km/h

Notes:

SPANISH GRAND PRIX - BARCELONA

Circuit Name : Circuit de Catalunya			Round 5 of 19
Number of Laps: **Total Distance:**	66 307.104 km · 190.825 miles	**Lap Record:** **F1 Car:**	Kimi Räikkönen Ferrari F2008
Circuit Length:	4.655 km · 2.892 miles	**Time · Date:**	1:21.670 · 27/04/2008
Web Site:	www.circuitcat.com	**Lap Speed:** **(average)**	205.192 km/h 127.493 mph
Address:	Circuit de Catalunya, Mas "La Moreneta", P O Box 27, 08160 Montmeló, Barcelona, Spain Telephone : +34 93 571 9700 · Fax : +34 93 572 2772		

Winners @ Circuit de Catalunya

Year · Driver · Constructor	Year · Driver · Constructor
2010 · Mark Webber · Red Bull-Renault	
2009 · Jenson Button · Brawn-Mercedes	
2008 · Kimi Räikkönen · Ferrari	
2007 · Felipe Massa · Ferrari	
2006 · Fernando Alonso · Renault	
2005 · Kimi Räikkönen · McLaren-Mercedes	
2004 · Michael Schumacher · Ferrari	
2003 · Michael Schumacher · Ferrari	
2002 · Michael Schumacher · Ferrari	
2001 · Michael Schumacher · Ferrari	
2000 · Mika Häkkinen · McLaren-Mercedes	
1999 · Mika Häkkinen · McLaren-Mercedes	
1998 · Mika Häkkinen · McLaren-Mercedes	
1997 · Jacques Villeneuve · Williams-Renault	
1996 · Michael Schumacher · Ferrari	
1995 · Michael Schumacher · Benetton-Renault	
1994 · Damon Hill · Williams-Renault	
1993 · Alain Prost · Williams-Renault	
1992 · Nigel Mansell · Williams-Renault	
1991 · Nigel Mansell · Williams-Renault	

Team Winners:	Benetton 1 · Brawn GP 1 · Ferrari 7 · McLaren 4 · Red Bull 1 · Renault 1 Williams 5

SPANISH GRAND PRIX - BARCELONA

Circuit Name : Circuit de Catalunya			20th to 22nd May 2011
Time Zone	GMT +1	Top Speed	~325 km/h • ~202 mph
Circuit Direction	Clockwise	Latitude	41° 34' 12" N
Capacity	107,000±	Longitude	2° 15' 40" E
Turns	16	Years GP Held	20

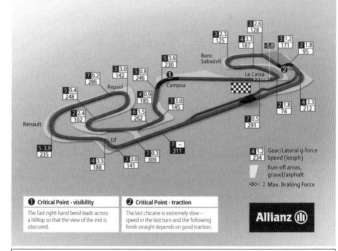

1 Critical Point - visibility
The fast right-hand bend leads across a hilltop so that the view of the exit is obscured.

2 Critical Point - traction
The last chicane is extremely slow – speed in the last turn and the following finish straight depends on good traction.

Gear/Lateral g-force
Speed (kmph)
Run-off areas, gravel/asphalt
Max. Braking Force

Allianz ⑪

2010 Circuit Results : Circuit de Catalunya

Position • Driver • Team/Engine • Time/Gap • Speed

Pole Position • Mark Webber • Red Bull-Renault • 1m 19.995s • 209.488 km/h
Fastest Lap • Lewis Hamilton • McLaren-Mercedes • 1m 24.357s • 198.655 km/h • On Lap 59

1st • Mark Webber • Red Bull-Renault • 1h 35m 44.101s • 192.471 km/h
2nd • Fernando Alonso • Ferrari • +24.065s • 191.668 km/h
3rd • Sebastian Vettel • Red Bull-Renault • +51.338s • 190.766 km/h

Notes:

MONACO GRAND PRIX - MONTE CARLO

Circuit Name : Circuit de Monaco			
Number of Laps: **Total Distance:**	78 260.520 km · 161.887 miles	**Lap Record:** **F1 Car:**	Michael Schumacher Ferrari F2004
Circuit Length:	3.340 km · 2.075 miles	**Time · Date:**	1:14.439 · 23/05/2004
Web Site:	www.acm.mc	**Lap Speed:** **(average)**	161.527 km/h 100.373 mph
Address:	Automobile Club de Monaco, 23 Boulevard Albert 1er, BP 464, MC-98000, Monaco Telephone : +377 931 52600 · Fax : +377 932 58008		

Winners @ Circuit de Monaco

Year · Driver · Constructor	Year · Driver · Constructor
2010 · Mark Webber · Red Bull-Renault	1976 · Niki Lauda · Ferrari
2009 · Jenson Button · Brawn-Mercedes	1975 · Niki Lauda · Ferrari
2008 · Lewis Hamilton · McLaren-Mercedes	1974 · Ronnie Peterson · Lotus-Ford
2007 · Fernando Alonso · Renault	1973 · Jacky Stewart · Tyrrell-Ford
2006 · Fernando Alonso · McLaren-Mercedes	1972 · Jean-Pierre Beltoise · BRM
2005 · Kimi Räikkönen · McLaren-Mercedes	1971 · Jacky Stewart · Tyrrell-Ford
2004 · Jarno Trulli · Renault	1970 · Jochen Rindt · Lotus-Ford
2003 · Juan Pablo Montoya · Williams-BMW	1969 · Graham Hill · Lotus-Ford
2002 · David Coulthard · McLaren-Mercedes	1968 · Graham Hill · Lotus-Ford
2001 · Michael Schumacher · Ferrari	1967 · Denny Hulme · Brabham-Repco
2000 · David Coulthard · McLaren-Mercedes	1966 · Jacky Stewart · BRM
1999 · Michael Schumacher · Ferrari	1965 · Graham Hill · BRM
1998 · Mika Häkkinen · McLaren-Mercedes	1964 · Graham Hill · BRM
1997 · Michael Schumacher · Ferrari	1963 · Graham Hill · BRM
1996 · Olivier Panis · Ligier-Mugen	1962 · Bruce McLaren · Cooper-Climax
1995 · Michael Schumacher · Benetton-Renault	1961 · Stirling Moss · Lotus-Climax
1994 · Michael Schumacher · Benetton-Renault	1960 · Stirling Moss · Mercedes-Benz
1993 · Ayrton Senna · McLaren-Ford	1959 · Jack Brabham · Cooper-Climax
1992 · Ayrton Senna · McLaren-Ford	1958 · Maurice Trintignant · Cooper-Climax
1991 · Ayrton Senna · McLaren-Honda	1957 · Juan-Manuel Fangio · Maserati
1990 · Ayrton Senna · McLaren-Honda	1956 · Stirling Moss · Maserati
1989 · Ayrton Senna · McLaren-Honda	1955 · Maurice Trintignant · Ferrari
1988 · Alain Prost · McLaren-Honda	1954 · *Race Not Held*
1987 · Ayrton Senna · McLaren-Honda	1953 · *Race Not Held*
1986 · Alain Prost · McLaren-TAG (Porsche)	1952 · *Non-championship Race*
1985 · Alain Prost · McLaren-TAG (Porsche)	1951 · *Race Not Held*
1984 · Alain Prost · McLaren-TAG (Porsche)	1950 · Juan-Manuel Fangio · Alfa Romeo
1983 · Keke Rosberg · Williams-Ford	
1982 · Riccardo Patrese · Brabham-Ford	
1981 · Gilles Villeneuve · Ferrari	
1980 · Carlos Reutermann · Williams-Ford	
1979 · Jody Scheckter · Ferrari	
1978 · Patrick Depailler · Tyrrell-Ford	
1977 · Niki Lauda · Ferrari	

Team Winners:	Alfa Romeo 1 · Benetton 2 · Brabham 2 · Brawn GP 1 · BRM 5 · Cooper 3 Ferrari 9 · Ligier 1 · Lotus 5 · Maserati 2 · Mercedes-Benz 1 · McLaren 16 Red Bull 1 · Renault 2 · Tyrrell 3 · Williams 3

MONACO GRAND PRIX - MONTE CARLO

Circuit Name : Circuit de Monaco		26th & 28th to 29th May 2011	
Time Zone	GMT +1	**Top Speed**	~305 km/h · ~190 mph
Circuit Direction	Clockwise	**Latitude**	43° 44' 5" N
Capacity	120,000±	**Longitude**	7° 25' 14" E
Turns	19	**Years GP Held**	57

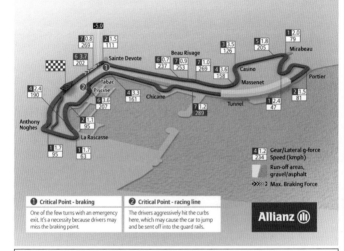

① Critical Point - braking

One of the few turns with an emergency exit. It's a necessity because drivers may miss the braking point.

② Critical Point - racing line

The drivers aggressively hit the curbs here, which may cause the car to jump and be sent off into the guard rails.

Allianz ⑪

2010 Circuit Results : Circuit de Monaco

Position · Driver · Team/Engine · Time/Gap · Speed

Pole Position · Mark Webber · Red Bull-Renault · 1m 13.826s · 162.869 km/h
Fastest Lap · Sebastian Vettel · Red Bull-Renault · 1m 15.192s · 159.910 km/h · On Lap 71

1st · Mark Webber · Red Bull-Renault · 1h 50m 13.355s · 141.814 km/h
2nd · Sebastian Vettel · Red Bull-Renault · +0.448s · 141.805 km/h
3rd · Robert Kubica · Renault · +1.675s · 141.778 km/h

Notes:

CANADIAN GRAND PRIX - MONTRÉAL

Circuit Name : Circuit Gilles Villeneuve			Round 7 of 19

Number of Laps: Total Distance:	70 305.270 km • 189.694 miles	Lap Record: F1 Car:	Rubens Barrichello Ferrari F2004
Circuit Length:	4.361 km • 2.710 miles	Time • Date:	1:13.622 • 13/06/2004
Web Site:	www.circuitgillesvilleneuve.ca	Lap Speed: (average)	213.246 km/h 132.511 mph
Address:	222 Circuit Gilles-Villeneuve, Parc Jean-Drapeau, Montréal, Québec, H3C 6A1, Canada Telephone : +1 514 350 0000 • Fax : +1 514 350 0007		

Winners @ Circuit Gilles Villeneuve

Year • Driver • Constructor	Year • Driver • Constructor
2010 • Mark Webber • Red Bull-Renault	
2009 • *Race Not Held*	
2008 • Robert Kubica • BMW-Sauber	
2007 • Lewis Hamilton • McLaren-Mercedes	
2006 • Fernando Alonso • Renault	
2005 • Kimi Räikkönen • McLaren-Mercedes	
2004 • Michael Schumacher • Ferrari	
2003 • Michael Schumacher • Ferrari	
2002 • Michael Schumacher • Ferrari	
2001 • Ralf Schumacher • Williams-BMW	
2000 • Michael Schumacher • Ferrari	
1999 • Mika Häkkinen • McLaren-Mercedes	
1998 • Michael Schumacher • Ferrari	
1997 • Michael Schumacher • Ferrari	
1996 • Damon Hill • Williams-Renault	
1995 • Jean Alesi • Ferrari	
1994 • Michael Schumacher • Benetton-Ford	
1993 • Alain Prost • Williams-Renault	
1992 • Gerhard Berger • McLaren-Honda	
1991 • Nelson Piquet • Benetton-Ford	
1990 • Alan Jones • McLaren-Honda	
1989 • Thierry Boutsen • Williams-Renault	
1988 • Alan Jones • McLaren-Honda	
1987 • *Race Not Held*	
1986 • Nigel Mansell • Williams-Honda	
1985 • Michele Alboreto • Ferrari	
1984 • Nelson Piquet • Brabham-BMW	
1983 • René Arnoux • Ferrari	
1982 • Nelson Piquet • Brabham-BMW	
1981 • Jacques Laffite • Ligier-Matra	
1980 • Ayrton Senna • Williams-Ford	
1979 • Ayrton Senna • Williams-Ford	
1978 • Gilles Villeneuve • Ferrari	

Team Winners:	Benetton 2 • BMW 1 • Brabham 2 • Ferrari 10 • Ligier 1 • McLaren 6 Red Bull 1 • Renault 1 • Williams 7

CANADIAN GRAND PRIX - MONTRÉAL

Circuit Name : Circuit Gilles Villeneuve			10th to 12th June 2011
Time Zone	GMT –5	Top Speed	~348 km/h • ~216 mph
Circuit Direction	Clockwise	Latitude	45° 30' 21" N
Capacity	100,000±	Longitude	73° 31' 36" W
Turns	15	Years GP Held	31

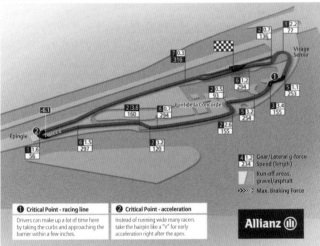

① Critical Point - racing line

Drivers can make up a lot of time here by taking the curbs and approaching the barrier within a few inches.

② Critical Point - acceleration

Instead of running wide many racers take the hairpin like a "V" for early acceleration right after the apex.

Allianz ⑪

2010 Circuit Results : Circuit Gilles Villeneuve

Position • Driver • Team/Engine • Time/Gap • Speed

Pole Position • Lewis Hamilton • McLaren-Mercedes • 1m 15.105s • 209.035 km/h
Fastest Lap • Robert Kubica • Renault • 1m 16.972s • 203.965 km/h • On Lap 67

1st • Lewis Hamilton • McLaren-Mercedes • 1h 33m 53.456s • 195.079 km/h
2nd • Jenson Button • McLaren-Mercedes • +2.254s • 195.001 km/h
3rd • Fernando Alonso • Ferrari • +9.214s • 194.760 km/h

Notes:

EUROPEAN GRAND PRIX - VALENCIA

Circuit Name : Valencia Street Circuit			Round 8 of 19
Number of Laps: **Total Distance:**	57 308.883 km · 191.919 miles	**Lap Record:** **F1 Car:**	Timo Glock Toyota RVX-09
Circuit Length:	5.419 km · 3.367 miles	**Time · Date:**	1:38.683 · 23/08/2009
Web Site:	www.valenciastreetcircuit.com	**Lap Speed:** **(average)**	197.688 km/h 112.843 mph
Address:	Valencia Street Circuit, Calle Doctor Lluch, 4, 46011 Valencia, Spain		
	Telephone : +34 96 316 40 07 · Fax : +34 96 367 87 60		

Winners @ Valencia Street Circuit

Year · Driver · Constructor	Year · Driver · Constructor
2010 · Sebastian Vettel · Red Bull-Renault 2009 · Rubens Barrichello · Brawn-Mercedes 2008 · Felipe Massa · Ferrari	

Team Winners:	Brawn GP 1 · Ferrari 1 · Red Bull 1

EUROPEAN GRAND PRIX - VALENCIA

Circuit Name : Valencia Street Circuit		24th to 26th June 2011	
Time Zone	GMT +1	Top Speed	~300 km/h ~ ~186 mph
Circuit Direction	Clockwise	Latitude	50° 19' 51.6" N
Capacity	120,000±	Longitude	6° 56' 34.8" E
Turns	25	Years GP Held	3

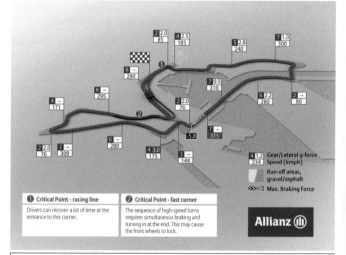

① **Critical Point - racing line**
Drivers can recover a lot of time at the entrance to this corner.

② **Critical Point - fast corner**
The sequence of high-speed turns requires simultaneous braking and turning in at the end. This may cause the front wheels to lock.

Gear/Lateral g-force
Speed (kmph)
Run-off areas, gravel/asphalt
Max. Braking Force

Allianz ⑪

2010 Circuit Results : Valencia Street Circuit

Position · Driver · Team/Engine · Time/Gap · Speed

Pole Position · Sebastian Vettel · Red Bull-Renault · 1m 37.587s · 199.907 km/h
Fastest Lap · Jenson Button · McLaren-Mercedes · 1m 38.766s · 197.521 km/h · On Lap 54

1st · Sebastian Vettel · Red Bull-Renault · 1h 40m 29.571s · 184.420 km/h
2nd · Lewis Hamilton · McLaren-Mercedes · +5.042s · 184.266 km/h
3rd · Jenson Button · McLaren-Mercedes · +12.658s · 184.034 km/h

Notes:

BRITISH GRAND PRIX - SILVERSTONE

Circuit Name : Silverstone Circuit (New Circuit Layout)			Round 9 of 19
Number of Laps: **Total Distance:**	52 306.227 km • 190.280 miles	**Lap Record:** **F1 Car:**	Fernando Alonso Ferrari F10
Circuit Length:	5.891 km • 3.660 miles	**Time • Date:**	1:30.874 • 11/07/2010
Web Site:	www.silverstone.co.uk	**Lap Speed:** **(average)**	233.374 km/h 145.011 mph
Address:	Silverstone Circuit Ltd, Silverstone, Towcester, Northamptonshire, NN12 8TN, United Kingdom Telephone : +44 (0) 8704 588 200 • Fax : +44 (0) 8704 588 250		

Winners @ Silverstone Circuit

Year • Driver • Constructor	Year • Driver • Constructor
2010 • Mark Webber • Red Bull-Renault	1976 • *Race Not Held - Brands Hatch*
2009 • Sebastian Vettel • Red Bull-Renault	1975 • Emerson Fittipaldi • McLaren-Cosworth
2008 • Lewis Hamilton • McLaren-Mercedes	1974 • *Race Not Held - Brands Hatch*
2007 • Kimi Räikkönen • Ferrari	1973 • Peter Revson • McLaren-Cosworth
2006 • Fernando Alonso • Renault	1972 • *Race Not Held - Brands Hatch*
2005 • Juan Pablo Montoya • McLaren-Mercedes	1971 • Jackie Stewart • Tyrrell-Cosworth
2004 • Michael Schumacher • Ferrari	1970 • *Race Not Held - Brands Hatch*
2003 • Rubens Barrichello • Ferrari	1969 • Jackie Stewart • Matra-Cosworth
2002 • Michael Schumacher • Ferrari	1968 • *Race Not Held - Brands Hatch*
2001 • Mika Häkkinen • McLaren-Mercedes	1967 • Jim Clark • Lotus-Cosworth
2000 • David Coulthard • McLaren-Mercedes	1966 • *Race Not Held - Brands Hatch*
1999 • David Coulthard • McLaren-Mercedes	1965 • Jim Clark • Lotus-Climax
1998 • Michael Schumacher • Ferrari	1964 • *Race Not Held - Brands Hatch*
1997 • Jacques Villeneuve • Williams-Renault	1963 • Jim Clark • Lotus-Climax
1996 • Jacques Villeneuve • Williams-Renault	1962 • *Race Not Held - Aintree*
1995 • Johnny Herbert • Benetton-Renault	1961 • *Race Not Held - Aintree*
1994 • Damon Hill • Williams-Renault	1960 • Jack Brabham • Cooper-Climax
1993 • Alain Prost • Williams-Renault	1959 • *Race Not Held - Aintree*
1992 • Nigel Mansell • Williams-Renault	1958 • Peter Collins • Ferrari
1991 • Nigel Mansell • Williams-Renault	1957 • *Race Not Held - Aintree*
1990 • Alain Prost • Ferrari	1956 • Juan-Manuel Fangio • Lancia-Ferrari
1989 • Alain Prost • McLaren-Honda	1955 • *Race Not Held - Aintree*
1988 • Ayrton Senna • McLaren-Honda	1954 • José Froilán González • Ferrari
1987 • Nigel Mansell • Williams-Honda	1953 • Alberto Ascari • Ferrari
1986 • *Race Not Held - Brands Hatch*	1952 • Alberto Ascari • Ferrari
1985 • Alain Prost • McLaren-TAG (Porsche)	1951 • José Froilán González • Ferrari
1984 • *Race Not Held - Brands Hatch*	1950 • Giuseppe Farina • Alfa Romeo
1983 • Alain Prost • Renault	
1982 • *Race Not Held - Brands Hatch*	
1981 • John Watson • McLaren-Cosworth	
1980 • *Race Not Held - Brands Hatch*	
1979 • Clay Regazzoni • Williams-Cosworth	
1978 • *Race Not Held - Brands Hatch*	
1977 • James Hunt • McLaren-Cosworth	

Team Winners:	Alfa Romeo 1 • Benetton 1 • Cooper 1 • Ferrari 11 • Lancia 1 • Lotus 3 • Matra 1 McLaren 12 • Red Bull 2 • Renault 2 • Tyrrell 1 • Williams 8

BRITISH GRAND PRIX - SILVERSTONE

Circuit Name : Silverstone Circuit (New Circuit Layout)			8th to 10th July 2011
Time Zone	GMT +0	**Top Speed**	~335 km/h · ~205 mph
Circuit Direction	Clockwise	**Latitude**	52° 4' 43" N
Capacity	120,000±	**Longitude**	1° 1' 1" W
Turns	18	**Years GP Held**	44

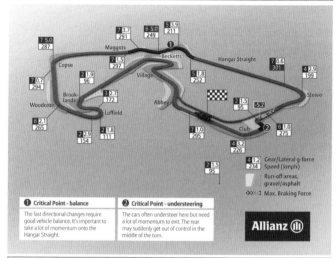

❶ Critical Point - balance

The fast directional changes require good vehicle balance. It's important to take a lot of momentum onto the Hangar Straight.

❷ Critical Point - understeering

The cars often understeer here but need a lot of momentum to exit. The rear may suddenly get out of control in the middle of the turn.

Allianz ⑪

2010 Circuit Results : Silverstone Circuit

Position · Driver · Team/Engine · Time/Gap · Speed

Pole Position · Sebastian Vettel · Red Bull-Renault · 1m 29.615s · 236.652 km/h
Fastest Lap · Fernando Alonso · Ferrari · 1m 30.874s · 233.373 km/h · On Lap 52

1st · Mark Webber · Red Bull-Renault · 1h 24m 38.200s · 217.088 km/h
2nd · Lewis Hamilton · McLaren-Mercedes · +1.360s · 217.030 km/h
3rd · Nico Rosberg · Mercedes · +21.307s · 216.181 km/h

Notes:

GERMAN GRAND PRIX - NÜRBURGRING

Circuit Name : Nürburgring			Round 10 of 19
Number of Laps: **Total Distance:**	60 308.863 km · 191.938 miles	**Lap Record:** **F1 Car:**	Michael Schumacher Ferrari F2004
Circuit Length:	5.148 km · 3.199 miles	**Time · Date:**	1:29.468 · 30/05/2004
Web Site:	www.nuerburgring.de	**Lap Speed:** **(average)**	207.144 km/h 138.685 mph
Address:	Nürburgring Automotive GmbH, Nürburgring Boulevard 1, 53520 Nürburg Germany Telephone : +49 (0) 26 91 / 30 2 - 0 · Fax : +49 (0) 26 91 / 30 2 - 155		

Winners @ Nürburgring

Year · Driver · Constructor	Year · Driver · Constructor
2010 · *Race Not Held - Hockenheimring*	1976 · James Hunt · McLaren-Ford
2009 · Mark Webber · Red Bull-Renault	1975 · Carlos Reutemann · Brabham-Ford
2008 · *Race Not Held - Hockenheimring*	1974 · Clay Regazzoni · Ferrari
2007 · Fernando Alonso · McLaren-Mercedes	1973 · Jackie Stewart · Tyrrell-Ford
2006 · Michael Schumacher · Ferrari	1972 · Jacky Ickx · Ferrari
2005 · Fernando Alonso · Renault	1971 · Jackie Stewart · Tyrrell-Ford
2004 · Michael Schumacher · Ferrari	1970 · *Race Not Held - Hockenheimring*
2003 · Ralf Schumacher · Williams-BMW	1969 · Jacky Ickx · Brabham-Ford
2002 · Rubens Barrichello · Ferrari	1968 · Jackie Stewart · Matra-Ford
2001 · Michael Schumacher · Ferrari	1967 · Denny Hulme · Brabham-Repco
2000 · Michael Schumacher · Ferrari	1966 · Jack Brabham · Brabham-Repco
1999 · Johnny Herbert · Stewart-Ford	1965 · Jim Clark · Lotus-Climax
1998 · Mika Häkkinen · McLaren-Mercedes	1964 · John Surtees · Ferrari
1997 · Jacques Villeneuve · Williams-Renault	1963 · John Surtees · Ferrari
1996 · Jacques Villeneuve · Williams-Renault	1962 · Graham Hill · BRM
1995 · Michael Schumacher · Benetton-Renault	1961 · Stirling Moss · Lotus-Climax
1994 · *Race Not Held - Hockenheimring*	1960 · *Non-Championship Race*
1993 · *Race Not Held - Hockenheimring*	1959 · *Race Not Held - AVUS Berlin*
1992 · *Race Not Held - Hockenheimring*	1958 · Tony Brooks · Vanwall
1991 · *Race Not Held - Hockenheimring*	1957 · Juan Manuel Fangio · Maserati
1990 · *Race Not Held - Hockenheimring*	1956 · Juan Manuel Fangio · Ferrari
1989 · *Race Not Held - Hockenheimring*	1955 · *Race Not Held*
1988 · *Race Not Held - Hockenheimring*	1954 · Juan Manuel Fangio · Mercedes-Benz
1987 · *Race Not Held - Hockenheimring*	1953 · Giuseppe Farina · Ferrari
1986 · *Race Not Held - Hockenheimring*	1952 · Alberto Ascari · Ferrari
1985 · Michele Alboreto · Ferrari	1951 · Alberto Ascari · Ferrari
1984 · Alain Prost · McLaren-TAG (Porsche)	
1983 · *Race Not Held - Hockenheimring*	
1982 · *Race Not Held - Hockenheimring*	
1981 · *Race Not Held - Hockenheimring*	
1980 · *Race Not Held - Hockenheimring*	
1979 · *Race Not Held - Hockenheimring*	
1978 · *Race Not Held - Hockenheimring*	
1977 · *Race Not Held - Hockenheimring*	

Team Winners:	Benetton 1 · Brabham 4 · BRM 1 · Ferrari 14 · Lotus 2 · Maserati 1 · Matra 1 McLaren 4 · Mercedes-Benz 1 · Red Bull 1 · Renault 1 · Stewart 1 · Tyrrell 2 Vanwall 1 · Williams 3

GERMAN GRAND PRIX - NÜRBURGRING

Circuit Name : Nürburgring			22nd to 24th July 2011
Time Zone	GMT +1	Top Speed	~300 km/h • ~186 mph
Circuit Direction	Clockwise	Latitude	50° 20' 08" N
Capacity	140,000±	Longitude	6° 56' 51" E
Turns	16	Years GP Held	38

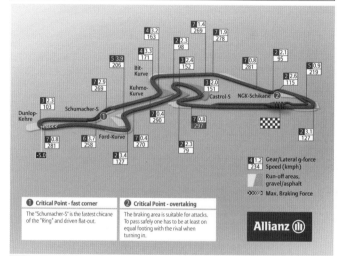

1 Critical Point - fast corner

The "Schumacher-S" is the fastest chicane of the "Ring" and driven flat-out.

2 Critical Point - overtaking

The braking area is suitable for attacks. To pass safely one has to be at least on equal footing with the rival when turning in.

Allianz (||)

2009 Circuit Results : Nürburgring

Position • Driver • Team/Engine • Time/Gap • Speed

Pole Position • Mark Webber • Red Bull-Renault • 1m 32.230s • 200.941 km/h
Fastest Lap • Fernando Alonso • Ferrari • 1m 33.365s • 198.498 km/h • On Lap 49

1st • Mark Webber • Red Bull-Renault • 1h 36m 43.310s • 191.598 km/h
2nd • Sebastian Vettel • Red Bull-Renault • +9.252s • 191.293 km/h
3rd • Felipe Massa • Ferrari • +15.906s • 191.074 km/h

Notes:

HUNGARIAN GRAND PRIX - BUDAPEST

Circuit Name : Hungaroring			Round 11 of 19
Number of Laps: **Total Distance:**	70 306.630 km · 190.539 miles	**Lap Record:** **F1 Car:**	Michael Schumacher Ferrari F2004
Circuit Length:	4.381 km · 2.722 miles	**Time · Date:**	1:19.071 · 15/08/2004
Web Site:	www.hungaroring.hu	**Lap Speed:** **(average)**	199.461 km/h 123.828 mph
Address:	Hungaroring Sport RT, PO Box 10, 2146 Mogyorod, Budapest, Hungary Telephone : +36 28 444 444 · Fax : +36 28 441 860		

Winners @ Hungaroring

Year · Driver · Constructor	Year · Driver · Constructor
2010 · Mark Webber · Red Bull-Renault	
2009 · Lewis Hamilton · McLaren-Mercedes	
2008 · Heikki Kovalainen · McLaren-Mercedes	
2007 · Lewis Hamilton · McLaren-Mercedes	
2006 · Jenson Button · Honda	
2005 · Kimi Räikkönen · McLaren-Mercedes	
2004 · Michael Schumacher · Ferrari	
2003 · Fernando Alonso · Renault	
2002 · Rubens Barrichello · Ferrari	
2001 · Michael Schumacher · Ferrari	
2000 · Mika Häkkinen · McLaren-Mercedes	
1999 · Mika Häkkinen · McLaren-Mercedes	
1998 · Michael Schumacher · Benetton-Ford	
1997 · Jacques Villeneuve · Williams-Renault	
1996 · Jacques Villeneuve · Williams-Renault	
1995 · Damon Hill · Williams-Renault	
1994 · Michael Schumacher · Benetton-Ford	
1993 · Damon Hill · Williams-Renault	
1992 · Ayrton Senna · McLaren-Honda	
1991 · Ayrton Senna · McLaren-Honda	
1990 · Thierry Boutsen · Williams-Renault	
1989 · Nigel Mansell · Ferrari	
1988 · Ayrton Senna · McLaren-Honda	
1987 · Nelson Piquet · Williams-Honda	
1986 · Nelson Piquet · Williams-Honda	

Team Winners:	Benetton 1 · Ferrari 5 · Honda 1 · McLaren 9 · Red Bull 1 · Renault 2 · Williams 6

HUNGARIAN GRAND PRIX - BUDAPEST

Circuit Name : Hungaroring			29th to 31st July 2011
Time Zone	GMT +1	Top Speed	~310 km/h · ~193 mph
Circuit Direction	Clockwise	Latitude	47° 34' 44" N
Capacity	120,000±	Longitude	19° 14' 55" E
Turns	14 (+ 2 Hairpins)	Years GP Held	25

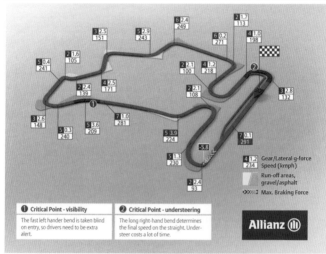

① Critical Point - visibility
The fast left hander bend is taken blind on entry, so drivers need to be extra alert.

② Critical Point - understeering
The long right-hand bend determines the final speed on the straight. Understeer costs a lot of time.

4 1.2 / 234 Gear/Lateral g-force Speed (kmph)

Run-off areas, gravel/asphalt

»»»⊃ Max. Braking Force

Allianz ⑪

2010 Circuit Results : Hungaroring

Position · Driver · Team/Engine · Time/Gap · Speed

Pole Position · Sebastian Vettel · Red Bull-Renault · 1m 18.773s · 200.215 km/h
Fastest Lap · Sebastian Vettel · Red Bull-Renault · 1m 22.362s · 191.491 km/h · On Lap 70

1st · Mark Webber · Red Bull-Renault · 1h 41m 05.571s · 181.989 km/h
2nd · Fernando Alonso · Ferrari · +17.821s · 181.455 km/h
3rd · Sebastian Vettel · Red Bull-Renault · +19.252s · 181.413 km/h

Notes:

BELGIAN GRAND PRIX - SPA

Circuit Name : Circuit de Spa-Francorchamps			Round 12 of 19
Number of Laps: **Total Distance:**	44 308.052 km · 191.410 miles	**Lap Record:** **F1 Car:**	Sebastian Vettel Red Bull Renault
Circuit Length:	7.004 km · 4.352 miles	**Time · Date:**	1:47.263 · 30/08/2009
Web Site:	www.spa-francorchamps.be	**Lap Speed:** **(average)**	235.058 km/h 146.065 mph
Address:	Circuit de Spa Francorchamps, Route du Circuit 55, B-4970 Francorchamps, Belgium Telephone : +32 87 29 37 00 · Fax : +32 87 27 05 81		

Winners @ Circuit de Spa-Francorchamps

Year · Driver · Constructor	Year · Driver · Constructor
2010 · Lewis Hamilton · McLaren-Mercedes	1976 · *Race held at Zolder*
2009 · Kimi Räikkönen · Ferrari	1975 · *Race held at Zolder*
2008 · Felipe Massa · Ferrari	1974 · *Race held at Nivelles*
2007 · Kimi Räikkönen · Ferrari	1973 · *Race held at Zolder*
2006 · *Race Not Held*	1972 · *Race held at Nivelles*
2005 · Kimi Räikkönen · McLaren-Mercedes	1971 · *Race Not Held*
2004 · Kimi Räikkönen · McLaren-Mercedes	1970 · Pedro Rodríguez · BRM
2003 · *Race Not Held*	1969 · *Race Not Held*
2002 · Michael Schumacher · Ferrari	1968 · Bruce McLaren · McLaren-Ford
2001 · Michael Schumacher · Ferrari	1967 · Dan Gurney · Eagle-Westlake
2000 · Mika Häkkinen · McLaren-Mercedes	1966 · John Surtees · Ferrari
1999 · David Coulthard · McLaren-Mercedes	1965 · Jim Clark · Lotus-Climax
1998 · Damon Hill · Jordan-Mugen Honda	1964 · Jim Clark · Lotus-Climax
1997 · Michael Schumacher · Ferrari	1963 · Jim Clark · Lotus-Climax
1996 · Michael Schumacher · Ferrari	1962 · Jim Clark · Lotus-Climax
1995 · Michael Schumacher · Benetton-Renault	1961 · Phil Hill · Ferrari
1994 · Damon Hill · McLaren–Renault	1960 · Jack Brabham · Cooper-Climax
1993 · Damon Hill · McLaren–Renault	1959 · *Race Not Held*
1992 · Michael Schumacher · Benetton-Ford	1958 · Tony Brooks · Vanwall
1991 · Ayrton Senna · McLaren-Honda	1957 · *Race Not Held*
1990 · Ayrton Senna · McLaren-Honda	1956 · Peter Collins · Ferrari
1989 · Ayrton Senna · McLaren-Honda	1955 · Juan-Manuel Fangio · Mercedes-Benz
1988 · Ayrton Senna · McLaren-Honda	1954 · Juan-Manuel Fangio · Maserati
1987 · Alain Prost · McLaren-TAG (Porsche)	1953 · Alberto Ascari · Ferrari
1986 · Nigel Mansell · Williams-Honda	1952 · Alberto Ascari · Ferrari
1985 · Ayrton Senna · Lotus-Renault	1951 · Giuseppe Farina · Alfa Romeo
1984 · *Race held at Zolder*	1950 · Juan-Manuel Fangio · Alfa Romeo
1983 · Alain Prost · Renault	
1982 · *Race held at Zolder*	
1981 · *Race held at Zolder*	
1980 · *Race held at Zolder*	
1979 · *Race held at Zolder*	
1978 · *Race held at Zolder*	
1977 · *Race held at Zolder*	

Team Winners:	Alfa Romeo 2 · Benetton 2 · BRM 1 · Cooper 1 · Eagle 1 · Ferrari 12 · Jordan 1 Lotus 5 · Maserati 1 · McLaren 14 · Mercedes-Benz 1 · Renault 1 · Vanwall 1

BELGIAN GRAND PRIX - SPA

Circuit Name : Circuit de Spa-Francorchamps			26th to 28th August 2011
Time Zone	GMT +1	Top Speed	~330 km/h • ~205 mph
Circuit Direction	Clockwise	Latitude	50° 26' 14" N
Capacity	80,000±	Longitude	5° 58' 17" E
Turns	21	Years GP Held	43

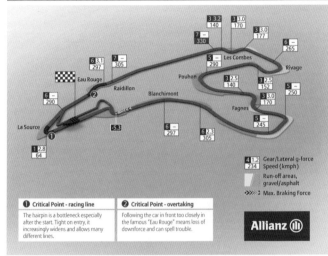

① Critical Point - racing line

The hairpin is a bottleneck especially after the start. Tight on entry, it increasingly widens and allows many different lines.

② Critical Point - overtaking

Following the car in front too closely in the famous "Eau Rouge" means loss of downforce and can spell trouble.

Allianz ⑪

2010 Circuit Results : Circuit de Spa-Francorchamps

Position • Driver • Team/Engine • Time/Gap • Speed

Pole Position • Mark Webber • Red Bull-Renault • 1m 45.778s • 238.370 km/h
Fastest Lap • Lewis Hamilton • McLaren-Mercedes • 1m 49.069s • 231.178 km/h • On Lap 32

1st • Lewis Hamilton • McLaren-Mercedes • 1h 29m 04.268s • 207.509 km/h
2nd • Mark Webber • Red Bull-Renault • +1.571s • 207.448 km/h
3rd • Robert Kubica • Renault • +4.771s • 207.374 km/h

Notes:

ITALIAN GRAND PRIX - MONZA

Circuit Name : Autodromo Nazionale Monza			Round 13 of 19
Number of Laps: **Total Distance:**	53 306.720 km · 190.596 miles	**Lap Record:** **F1 Car:**	Rubens Barrichello Ferrari F2004
Circuit Length:	5.793 km · 3.600 miles	**Time · Date:**	1:21.046 · 12/09/2004
Web Site:	www.monzanet.it	**Lap Speed:** **(average)**	257.321 km/h 159.899 mph
Address:	Autodromo Nazionale Monza, Parco Monza, 20052 Monza (MI), Italy Telephone : +39 39 24 821 · Fax : +39 39 32 0324		

Winners @ Autodromo Nazionale Monza

Year · Driver · Constructor	Year · Driver · Constructor
2010 · Fernando Alonso · Ferrari	1976 · Ronnie Peterson · March-Ford
2009 · Rubens Barrichello · Brawn-Mercedes	1975 · Clay Regazzoni · Ferrari
2008 · Sebastian Vettel · Toro Rosso-Ferrari	1974 · Ronnie Peterson · Lotus-Ford
2007 · Fernando Alonso · McLaren-Mercedes	1973 · Ronnie Peterson · Lotus-Ford
2006 · Michael Schumacher · Ferrari	1972 · Emerson Fittipaldi · Lotus-Ford
2005 · Juan Pablo Montoya · McLaren-Mercedes	1971 · Peter Gethin · BRM
2004 · Rubens Barrichello · Ferrari	1970 · Clay Regazzoni · Ferrari
2003 · Michael Schumacher · Ferrari	1969 · Jackie Stewart · Matra-Ford
2002 · Rubens Barrichello · Ferrari	1968 · Denny Hulme · McLaren-Ford
2001 · Juan Pablo Montoya · Williams-BMW	1967 · John Surtees · Honda
2000 · Michael Schumacher · Ferrari	1966 · Ludovico Scarfiotti · Ferrari
1999 · HH Frentzen · Jordan Mugen-Honda	1965 · Jackie Stewart · BRM
1998 · Michael Schumacher · Ferrari	1964 · John Surtees · Ferrari
1997 · David Coulthard · McLaren-Mercedes	1963 · Jim Clarke · Lotus-Climax
1996 · Michael Schumacher · Ferrari	1962 · Graham Hill · BRM
1995 · Johnny Herbert · Benetton-Renault	1961 · Phil Hill · Ferrari
1994 · Damon Hill · Williams-Renault	1960 · Phil Hill · Ferrari
1993 · Damon Hill · Williams-Renault	1959 · Stirling Moss · Cooper-Climax
1992 · Ayrton Senna · McLaren-Honda	1958 · Tony Brooks · Vanwall
1991 · Nigel Mansell · Williams-Renault	1957 · Stirling Moss · Vanwall
1990 · Ayrton Senna · McLaren-Honda	1956 · Stirling Moss · Maserati
1989 · Alain Prost · McLaren–Honda	1955 · Juan-Manuel Fangio · Mercedes-Benz
1988 · Gerhard Berger · Ferrari	1954 · Juan-Manuel Fangio · Mercedes-Benz
1987 · Nelson Piquet · Williams-Honda	1953 · Juan-Manuel Fangio · Maserati
1986 · Nelson Piquet · Williams-Honda	1952 · Alberto Ascari · Ferrari
1985 · Alain Prost · McLaren-TAG (Porsche)	1951 · Alberto Ascari · Ferrari
1984 · Niki Lauda · McLaren-TAG (Porsche)	1950 · Giuseppe Farina · Alfa Romeo
1983 · Nelson Piquet · Brabham-BMW	
1982 · René Arnoux · Renault	
1981 · Alain Prost · Renault	
1980 · *Race held at Imola*	
1979 · Jody Scheckter · Ferrari	
1978 · Niki Lauda · Brabham-Alfa Romeo	
1977 · Mario Andretti · Lotus-Ford	

Team Winners:	Alfa Romeo 1 · Benetton 1 · Brabham 2 · Brawn GP 1 · BRM 3 · Cooper 1 Ferrari 18 · Honda 1 · Jordan 1 · Lotus 5 · March 1 · Maserati 2 · Matra 1 McLaren 9 · Mercedes-Benz 2 · Renault 2 · Toro Rosso 1 · Vanwall · Williams 6

ITALIAN GRAND PRIX - MONZA

Circuit Name : Autodromo Nazionale Monza		9th to 11th September 2011	
Time Zone	GMT +1	**Top Speed**	~368 km/h • ~228 mph
Circuit Direction	Clockwise	**Latitude**	45° 37' 14" N
Capacity	114,000±	**Longitude**	9° 17' 22" E
Turns	11	**Years GP Held**	60

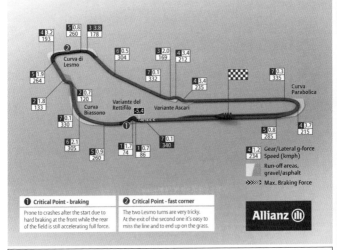

❶ Critical Point - braking	**❷ Critical Point - fast corner**
Prone to crashes after the start due to hard braking at the front while the rear of the field is still accelerating full force.	The two Lesmo turns are very tricky. At the exit of the second one it's easy to miss the line and to end up on the grass.

Allianz ⑪

2010 Circuit Results : Autodromo Nazionale Monza

Position • Driver • Team/Engine • Time/Gap • Speed

Pole Position • Fernando Alonso • Ferrari • 1m 29.962s • 254.444 km/h
Fastest Lap • Fernando Alonso • Ferrari • 1m 24.139s • 247.861 km/h • On Lap 52

1st • Fernando Alonso • Ferrari • 1h 16m 24.572s • 240.849 km/h
2nd • Jenson Button • McLaren-Mercedes • +2.938s • 240.695 km/h
3rd • Felipe Massa • Ferrari • +4.223s • 240.627 km/h

Notes:

SINGAPORE GRAND PRIX - MARINA BAY

Circuit Name : Marina Bay Street Circuit			Round 14 of 19
Number of Laps: **Total Distance:**	61 309.316 km · 192.208 miles	**Lap Record:** **F1 Car:**	Kimi Räikkönen Ferrari F2008
Circuit Length:	5.073 km · 3.152 miles	**Time · Date:**	1:45.599 · 28/09/2008
Web Site:	www.singaporegp.sg	**Lap Speed:** **(average)**	277.985 km/h 172.140 mph
Address:	Singapore GP Pte Ltd, 50 Cuscaden Road, #06-02 HPL House, Singapore 24972 Telephone : +65 6731 4982 · Fax : +65 6731 6032		

Winners @ Marina Bay Street Circuit

Year · Driver · Constructor	Year · Driver · Constructor
2010 · Fernando Alonso · Ferrari 2009 · Lewis Hamilton · McLaren-Mercedes 2008 · Fernando Alonso · Renault	

Team Winners:	McLaren 1 · Red Bull 1 · Renault 1 (Night & Street Race)

SINGAPORE GRAND PRIX - MARINA BAY

Circuit Name : Marina Bay Street Circuit		23rd to 25th September 2011	
Time Zone	GMT +8	**Top Speed**	~300 km/h · ~186 mph
Circuit Direction	Anticlockwise	**Latitude**	1° 17' 29.05" N
Capacity	110,000±	**Longitude**	103° 51' 50.93" E
Turns	23	**Years GP Held**	3

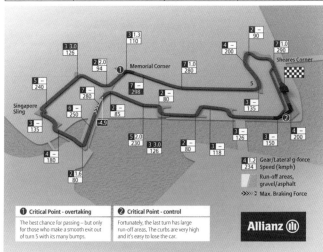

1 Critical Point - overtaking

The best chance for passing – but only for those who make a smooth exit out of turn 5 with its many bumps.

2 Critical Point - control

Fortunately, the last turn has large run-off areas. The curbs are very high and it's easy to lose the car.

Allianz ⑪

2010 Circuit Results : Marina Bay Street Circuit

Position · Driver · Team/Engine · Time/Gap · Speed

Pole Position · Fernando Alonso · Ferrari · 1m 45.390s · 173.287 km/h
Fastest Lap · Fernando Alonso · Ferrari · 1m 47.976s · 169.137 km/h · On Lap 58

1st · Fernando Alonso · Ferrari · 1h 57m 53.579s · 157.422 km/h
2nd · Sebastian Vettel · Red Bull-Renault · +0.293s · 157.415 km/h
3rd · Mark Webber · Red Bull-Renault · +29.141s · 156.776 km/h

Notes:

Circuit Name : Suzuka Circuit			Round 15 of 19
Number of Laps: **Total Distance:**	53 307 471 km - 191.062 miles	**Lap Record:** **F1 Car:**	Kimi Räikkönen McLaren MP4/20
Circuit Length:	5.807 km - 3.608 miles	**Time - Date:**	1:31.540 - 09/10/2005
Web Site:	www.mobilityland.co.jp	**Lap Speed:** **(average)**	228.372 km/h 141.904 mph
Address:	Mobilityland Corporation, 7992 Ino-cho, Suzuka-shi, Mie Prefecture, 510-0296, Japan Telephone : +81 (0) 3 3278 0777 - Fax : +81 (0) 3 3278 0733		

Winners @ Suzuka Circuit

Year - Driver - Constructor	Year - Driver - Constructor
2010 - Sebastian Vettel - Red Bull-Renault	1976 - *Race held at Fuji*
2009 - Sebastian Vettel - Red Bull-Renault	
2008 - *Race held at Fuji*	
2007 - *Race held at Fuji*	
2006 - Fernando Alonso - Renault	
2005 - Kimi Räikkönen - McLaren-Mercedes	
2004 - Michael Schumacher - Ferrari	
2003 - Rubens Barrichello - Ferrari	
2002 - Michael Schumacher - Ferrari	
2001 - Michael Schumacher - Ferrari	
2000 - Michael Schumacher - Ferrari	
1999 - Mika Häkkinen - McLaren Mercedes	
1998 - Mika Häkkinen - McLaren Mercedes	
1997 - Michael Schumacher - Ferrari	
1996 - Damon Hill - Williams-Renault	
1995 - Michael Schumacher - Benetton-Williams	
1994 - Damon Hill - Williams-Renault	
1993 - Ayrton Senna - McLaren-Ford	
1992 - Riccardo Patrese - Williams-Renault	
1991 - Gerhard Berger - McLaren-Honda	
1990 - Nelson Piquet - Benetton-Ford	
1989 - Alessandro Nannini - Ferrari	
1988 - Ayrton Senna - McLaren-Honda	
1987 - Gerhard Berger - Ferrari	
1986 - *Race Not Held*	
1985 - *Race Not Held*	
1984 - *Race Not Held*	
1983 - *Race Not Held*	
1982 - *Race Not Held*	
1981 - *Race Not Held*	
1980 - *Race Not Held*	
1979 - *Race Not Held*	
1978 - *Race Not Held*	
1977 - *Race held at Fuji*	

Team Winners:	Benetton 3 - Ferrari 7 - McLaren 6 - Red Bull 2 - Renault 1 - Williams 3

JAPANESE GRAND PRIX - SUZUKA

Circuit Name : Suzuka Circuit			7th to 9th October 2011
Time Zone	GMT +9	Top Speed	~310 km/h · ~192 mph
Circuit Direction	Clockwise	Latitude	34° 50' 35" N
Capacity	140,000±	Longitude	136° 32' 26" E
Turns	18	Years GP Held	22

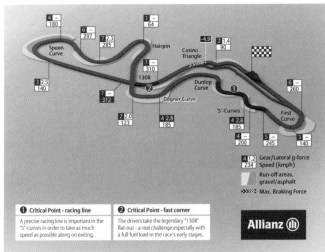

4 — 180	Spoon Curve	6 — 297	7 2.3 285		1 — 64 Hairpin	-4.9 Casino Triangle	2 1.4 90					

(Track diagram labels: 4 — 180, 6 — 297, 7 2.3 285, 1 — 64, Hairpin, -4.9, 2 1.4 90, 7 — 310 130R, Spoon Curve, Dunlop Curve, 6 — 260, 3 2.5 140, 7 — 312, Degner Curve, "S"-Curves, First Curve, 2 2.0 123, 4 2.8 185, 4 2.8 185, 4 — 200, 5 — 245, 3 — 140)

4 1.2 234 — Gear/Lateral g-force / Speed (kmph)

Run-off areas, gravel/asphalt

≫≫≫ Max. Braking Force

❶ Critical Point - racing line
A precise racing line is important in the "S"-curves in order to take as much speed as possible along on exiting.

❷ Critical Point - fast corner
The drivers take the legendary "130R" flat-out - a real challenge especially with a full fuel load in the race's early stages.

Allianz ⑪

2010 Circuit Results : Suzuka Circuit

Position · Driver · Team/Engine · Time/Gap · Speed

Pole Position · Sebastian Vettel · Red Bull-Renault · 1m 30.785s · 230.271 km/h
Fastest Lap · Mark Webber · Red Bull-Renault · 1m 33.474s · 223.647 km/h · On Lap 53

1st · Sebastian Vettel · Red Bull-Renault · 1h 30m 27.323s · 203.948 km/h
2nd · Mark Webber · Red Bull-Renault · +0.905s · 203.914 km/h
3rd · Fernando Alonso · Ferrari · +2.721s · 203.846 km/h

Notes:

KOREAN GRAND PRIX - YEONGAM

Number of Laps: **Total Distance:**	55 308.630 km · 191.773 miles	**Lap Record:** **F1 Car:**	Fernando Alonso Ferrari F10
Circuit Length:	5.615 km · 3.489 miles	**Time · Date:**	1:50.257 · 24/10/2010
Web Site:	www.koreangp.kr	**Lap Speed:** **(average)**	183.335 km/h 113.870 mph
Address:	Korean International Circuit, 12nd Floor, Mapo Tower, 418-1, Mapo-dong, Mapo-gu, Seoul, Korea 121-734 Telephone : +82 2 715 4646 · Fax : +82 2 715 6097		

Winners @ Korean International Circuit

Year · Driver · Constructor	Year · Driver · Constructor
2010 · Fernando Alonso · Ferrari	

Team Winners:	Ferrari 1

KOREAN GRAND PRIX - YEONGAM

Circuit Name : Korean International Circuit			14th to 16th October 2011
Time Zone	GMT +9	Top Speed	~315 km/h • ~195 mph
Circuit Direction	Anticlockwise	Latitude	34° 44' 0" N
Capacity	100,000±	Longitude	126° 25' 0" E
Turns	18	Years GP Held	1

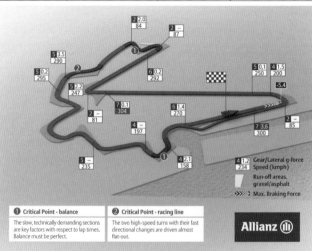

❶ Critical Point - balance

The slow, technically demanding sections are key factors with respect to lap times. Balance must be perfect.

❷ Critical Point - racing line

The two high-speed turns with their fast directional changes are driven almost flat-out.

Allianz (Ⅲ)

2010 Circuit Results : Korean International Circuit

Position • Driver • Team/Engine • Time/Gap • Speed

Pole Position • Sebastian Vettel • Red Bull-Renault • 1m 35.585s • 211.476 km/h
Fastest Lap • Fernando Alonso • Ferrari • 1m 50.257s • 183.335 km/h • On Lap 42

1st • Fernando Alonso • Ferrari • 2h 48m 20.810s • 109.997 km/h
2nd • Lewis Hamilton • McLaren-Mercedes • +14.999s • 109.834 km/h
3rd • Fernando Alonso • Ferrari • +30.868s • 109.662 km/h

Notes:

INDIAN GRAND PRIX - NEW DELHI

Circuit Name : Jaypee Group Circuit			Round 17 of 19
Number of Laps: **Total Distance:**	60 308.460 km · 191.668 miles	**Lap Record:** **F1 Car:**	n/a n/a
Circuit Length:	5.137 km · 3.192 miles	**Time · Date:**	n/a · n/a
Web Site:	http://www.jaypeesports.com/ motor-sport.shtml	**Lap Speed:** **(average)**	n/a km/h n/a mph
Address:	Jaypee Sports International Ltd. 2nd Floor, C-Block, Jaypee Greens Surajpur-Kasna Road, Greater Noida – 201310, India Telephone : +91 120 2326533		

Winners @ Jaypee Group Circuit

Year · Driver · Constructor	Year · Driver · Constructor
NEW CIRCUIT FOR 2011	

Team Winners:	

INDIAN GRAND PRIX - NEW DELHI

Circuit Name : Jaypee Group Circuit			28th to 30th October 2011
Time Zone	GMT +5.30	Top Speed	~ n/a km/h • ~ n/a mph
Circuit Direction	Clockwise	Latitude	28° 21' 02" N
Capacity	150,000±	Longitude	77° 32' 06" E
Turns	16	Years GP Held	0

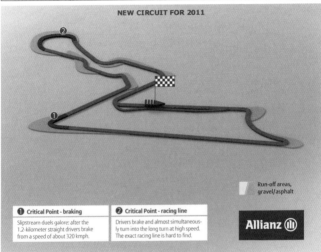

NEW CIRCUIT FOR 2011

Run-off areas, gravel/asphalt

❶ **Critical Point - braking**

Slipstream duels galore: after the 1.2-kilometer straight drivers brake from a speed of about 320 kmph.

❷ **Critical Point - racing line**

Drivers brake and almost simultaneously turn into the long turn at high speed. The exact racing line is hard to find.

Allianz ⑪

Notes:

ABU DHABI GRAND PRIX - YAS MARINA CIRCUIT

Circuit Name : Yas Marina Circuit			Round 18 of 19

Number of Laps: **Total Distance:**	55 305.355 km · 189.747 miles	**Lap Record:** **F1 Car:**	Sebastian Vettel Red Bull - Renault RB5
Circuit Length:	5.554 km · 3.451 miles	**Time · Date:**	1:40.279 · 01/11/2009
Web Site:	www.yasmarinacircuit.com	**Lap Speed:** **(average)**	199.377 km/h 123.893 mph
Address:	Yas Marina Circuit, P.O. Box 130001, Abu Dhabi, United Arab Emirates Telephone : +971 4 366 2125		

Winners @ Yas Marina Circuit

Year · Driver · Constructor	Year · Driver · Constructor
2010 · Sebastian Vettel · Red Bull-Renault 2009 · Sebastian Vettel · Red Bull-Renault	

Team Winners:	Red Bull 2

ABU DHABI GRAND PRIX - YAS MARINA CIRCUIT

Circuit Name : Yas Marina Circuit		11th to 13th November 2011	
Time Zone	GMT +4	Top Speed	~299 km/h • ~186 mph
Circuit Direction	Anticlockwise	Latitude	24° 28' 2" N
Capacity	50,000±	Longitude	54° 36' 11" E
Turns	21	Years GP Held	2

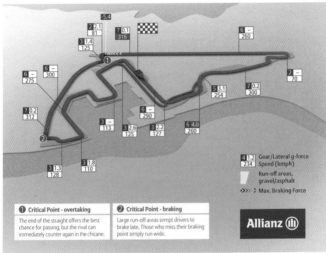

1 Critical Point - overtaking
The end of the straight offers the best chance for passing, but the rival can immediately counter again in the chicane.

2 Critical Point - braking
Large run-off areas tempt drivers to brake late. Those who miss their braking point simply run wide.

Allianz ⑪

2010 Circuit Results : Yas Marina Circuit

Position • Driver • Team/Engine • Time/Gap • Speed

Pole Position • Sebastian Vettel • Red Bull-Renault • 1m 39.394s • 201.163 km/h
Fastest Lap • Lewis Hamilton • McLaren-Mercedes • 1m 41.274s • 197.428 km/h • On Lap 47

1st • Sebastian Vettel • Red Bull-Renault • 1h 39m 36.837s • 183.923 km/h
2nd • Lewis Hamilton • McLaren-Mercedes • +10.162s • 183.610 km/h
3rd • Jenson Button • McLaren-Mercedes • +11.047s • 183.583 km/h

Notes:

BRAZILIAN GRAND PRIX - INTERLAGOS

Circuit Name : Autódromo José Carlos Pace			Round 19 of 19
Number of Laps: **Total Distance:**	71 305.909 km • 190.067 miles	**Lap Record:** **F1 Car:**	Juan Pablo Montoya Williams-BMW FW26
Circuit Length:	4.309 km • 2.677 miles	**Time • Date:**	1:11.473 • 24/10/2004
Web Site:	www.gpbrasil.com.br	**Lap Speed:** **(average)**	217.038 km/h 134.867 mph
Address:	Autódromo José Carlos Pace (Interlagos), Avenida Senador Teotonio Vilelia 267, São Paulo, Brazil Telephone : +55 11 504 13233 • Fax : +55 11 380 72996		

Winners @ Autódromo José Carlos Pace

Year • Driver • Constructor	Year • Driver • Constructor
2010 • Sebastian Vettel • Red Bull-Renault	1976 • Niki Lauda • Ferrari
2009 • Mark Webber • Red Bull-Renault	1975 • Carlos Pace • Brabham-Ford
2008 • Felipe Massa • Ferrari	1974 • Emerson Fittipaldi • McLaren-Ford
2007 • Kimi Räikkönen • Ferrari	1973 • Emerson Fittipaldi • Lotus-Ford
2006 • Felipe Massa • McLaren-Mercedes	1972 • *Non-Championship Race*
2005 • Juan Pablo Montoya • McLaren-Mercedes	
2004 • Juan Pablo Montoya • Williams-BMW	
2003 • Giancarlo Fisichella • Jordan-Ford	
2002 • Michael Schumacher • Ferrari	
2001 • David Coulthard • McLaren-Mercedes	
2000 • Michael Schumacher • Ferrari	
1999 • Mika Häkkinen • McLaren-Mercedes	
1998 • Mika Häkkinen • McLaren-Mercedes	
1997 • Jacques Villeneuve • Williams-Renault	
1996 • Damon Hill • Williams-Renault	
1995 • Michael Schumacher • Benetton-Renault	
1994 • Michael Schumacher • Benetton-Ford	
1993 • Ayrton Senna • McLaren-Ford	
1992 • Nigel Mansell • Williams-Renault	
1991 • Ayrton Senna • McLaren-Honda	
1990 • Alain Prost • Ferrari	
1989 • *Race held at Jacarepaguá*	
1988 • *Race held at Jacarepaguá*	
1987 • *Race held at Jacarepaguá*	
1986 • *Race held at Jacarepaguá*	
1985 • *Race held at Jacarepaguá*	
1984 • *Race held at Jacarepaguá*	
1983 • *Race held at Jacarepaguá*	
1982 • *Race held at Jacarepaguá*	
1981 • *Race held at Jacarepaguá*	
1980 • René Arnoux • Renault	
1979 • Jacques Laffite • Ligier-Ford	
1978 • *Race held at Jacarepaguá*	
1977 • Carlos Reutemann • Ferrari	

Team Winners:	Benetton 2 • Brabham 1 • Ferrari 7 • Jordan 1 • Ligier 1 • Lotus 1 • McLaren 8 Red Bull 2 • Renault 1 • Williams 4

Circuit Name : Autódromo José Carlos Pace		25th to 27th November 2011	
Time Zone	GMT −3	Top Speed	~325 km/h • ~202 mph
Circuit Direction	Anticlockwise	Latitude	23° 42' 13" S
Capacity	80,000±	Longitude	46° 41' 59" W
Turns	15	Years GP Held	28

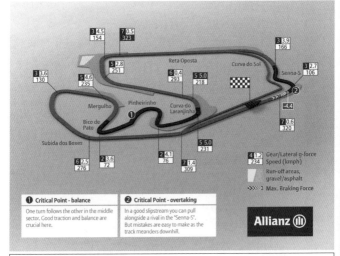

❶ Critical Point - balance

One turn follows the other in the middle sector. Good traction and balance are crucial here.

❷ Critical Point - overtaking

In a good slipstream you can pull alongside a rival in the "Senna-S". But mistakes are easy to make as the track meanders downhill.

Allianz ⑪

2010 Circuit Results : Autódromo José Carlos Pace

Position • Driver • Team/Engine • Time/Gap • Speed

Pole Position • Nico Hülkenberg • Williams-Cosworth • 1m 14.470s • 208.304 km/h
Fastest Lap • Lewis Hamilton • McLaren-Mercedes • 1m 13.851s • 210.049 km/h • On Lap 66

1st • Sebastian Vettel • Red Bull-Renault • 1h 33m 11.803s • 196.944 km/h
2nd • Mark Webber • Red Bull-Renault • +4.243s • 196.794 km/h
3rd • Fernando Alonso • Ferrari • +6.807s • 196.704 km/h

Notes:

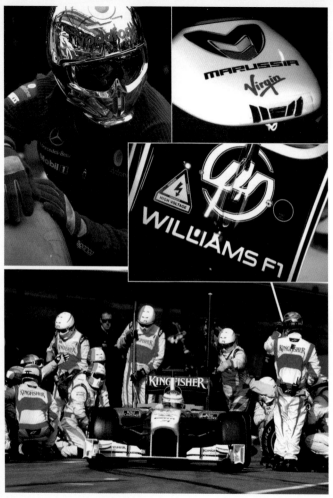

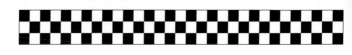

2011 REGULATIONS

DRIVER RACE WEAR

RACING FLAGS

RACING TERMS

ADDITIONAL DRIVER INFORMATION

ROBERT KUBICA

BAHRAIN CIRCUIT

FOLLOW THEM . . .

2011 - FORMULA 1 REGULATION CHANGES

Tyres

Pirelli takes over from Bridgestone as the sport's sole tyre supplier from 2011 to 2013. The tyre allocation for each driver remains at 11 sets of dry tyres per race weekend. Three sets (two prime & one option) can be used in P1 and P2 with one set returned after each session. A further eight sets can then be used for the rest of the weekend with one set of each specification handed back after qualifying. Each driver must use both specifications of dry tyres during a dry race. *See page 56 & 104*

Pirelli Tyre Colour Codes:

Intermediates	Rain/Wet	Hard Slicks	Supersoft Slicks	Soft Slicks	Medium Slicks

KERS

First introduced in 2009, KERS (Kinetic Energy Recovery System) returns to the sport in 2011 after the teams mutually agreed to suspend its use in 2010. KERS uses the energy generated under braking and makes it available to the driver through a boost button on the steering wheel. The button, which provides up to 60kW for around 6.6 seconds, can be used in one go or at different points around the lap. The minimum weight of the car including driver has now increased to 640kg to avoid penalising heavier drivers.

Adjustable Rear Wings (DRS - Drag Reduction System)

Drivers are now able to adjust the rear wing from the cockpit under new moveable bodywork regulations designed to improve overtaking. The system is electronically governed and can be used at any time during practice and qualifying but can only be activated during the race when the driver is one second or less behind another car at specific points on the track. The adjustable rear wing is automatically disabled if the driver uses the brakes.

Ban on F-Ducts & Double Diffusers

A new regulation prohibits any driver-influenced aerodynamic devices (with the exception of the adjustable rear wing) which means no F-ducts. Tightening of the regulations relating to the floor of the vehicle means double diffusers are also effectively banned. The height of the diffuser has been reduced from 175mm to 125mm.

107% Qualifying

2011 will see the return of a qualifying regulation not seen since 2002. The rule requires all drivers to finish with a time within 107% of the fastest driver in Q1 or they will not be allowed to race. The stewards will be authorised to allow drivers who don't qualify within this time to still race in certain circumstances at their discretion.

Curfew

A curfew has been introduced for team personnel associated with the operation of the cars who will not be allowed in the circuit during a six-hour period which commences ten hours before the scheduled start times of P1 on Friday and P3 on Saturday. Each team is permitted four individual exceptions to this rule during the season.

Penalties

Stewards can now impose a wider range of penalties for driving and other rule transgressions. The new penalties include: time penalties, exclusion from race results or suspension from subsequent events.

Wheel Tethers

A second tether must now be placed on every wheel to improve safety and reduce the risk of stray wheels.

Gearboxes

Gearboxes now need to last for five race weekends, instead of four race weekends as in 2010.

Team Orders

One very controversial area of the sport over the last few years has been the clause in the FIA regulations which governs team orders. There has been much speculation as to whether this rule has been adhered to, or whether the teams simply found a way to circumvent it; regardless, as of this year the clause has been removed.

DRIVER RACE WEAR

NOMEX®
Artificial fibre which undergoes thermal testing in the laboratory. It is subjected to an open flame with a temperature of 300 to 400 degrees Celsius that acts on the material from a distance of 3 cm. the drivers and pit crews underwear, socks and gloves are also made from NOMEX®.

BALACLAVA
Fireproof face mask made of NOMEX®, a flame retardant synthetic fibre. It's worn under the helmet.

OVERALL
Protective suit with elastic cuffs on the wrists and ankles made of two to four layers of NOMEX®. A completed multi layered overall undergoes 15 washings as well as a further 15 dry cleaning processes before it is finally tested. It is subjected to tempertures of 600 to 800 degrees Celsius.

GLOVES
Like the racing overalls, there are made of NOMEX®. The closefitting gloves with suede leather palms provide the necessary sensitivity for steering and ajusting buttons on the steering wheel.

UNDERWEAR
Under the racing overall, drivers wear a t-shirt, boxers, socks and a balaclava. All the underwear is made of fire resistant NOMEX® material.

BOOTS
Racing shoes are ankle boot's made of soft, cushioned leather. They have thin rubber soles with good grip to prevent the drivers feet from slipping off the pedals.

HELMET
The helmet is made of carbon, polyethylene and Kevlar®, it weighs approximately 1,300 grams. Like the car, it's designed in a wind tunnel to reduce drag as much as possiable. Helmets are subject to extreme deformation and fragmentation tests. Only helmets tested and authorised by the FIA may be used in races.

HEAD AND NECK SUPPORT (HANS®)
Since 2003, the drivers have been given additional head & neck protection system. The Head And Neck Support system, which consists of a carbon shoulder corset that connected to the safety belts and the driver's helmet. In case of an accident, HANS® is intended to prevent a stretching of the vertebrae. Additionally, it prevents the driver's head from hitting the steering wheel.

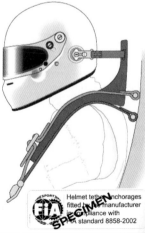

APPROVAL
All race wear must be approved by the FIA and conform to all the safety standards, to ensure the safety of the drivers and mechanics.

FIA STANDARDS
Helmet 8860-2004 (26th October 2005)
Protective Clothing 8856-2000 (30th June 2005)
HANS® System 8858-2002 (28th July 2005)
Safety Harnesses 8853/98 (1st January 2007)
Safety Harnesses 8854/98 (26th June 2002)

Helmet tether anchorages fitted by the manufacturer in compliance with FIA standard 8858-2002

RED FLAG
This flag should be waved at the start line when it has been decided to stop a practice session or the race. Simultaneously, each observer's post around the circuit should also wave a red flag.

The red flag may also be used by the Clerk of the Course or his nominee to close the circuit.

YELLOW FLAG
This is a signal of danger and should be shown to drivers in two ways with the following meanings:

Single waved: Reduce your speed, do not overtake and be prepared to change direction. There is a hazard beside or partly on the track.

Double waved: Reduce your speed, do not overtake and be prepared to change direction or stop. There is a hazard wholly or partly blocking the track.

Yellow flags should normally be shown only at the marshals' post immediately preceding the hazard. In some cases however the Clerk of the Course may order them to be shown at more than one marshals' post preceding an incident. Overtaking is not permitted between the first yellow flag and the green flag displayed after the incident.

Yellow flags should not be shown in the pit lane unless there is an incident of which the driver should be made aware.

BLACK FLAG
This flag should be used to inform the driver concerned that he must stop at his pit or at the place designated in the supplementary or championship regulations on the next approach to the pit entry. If a driver fails to comply for any reason, this flag should not be shown for more than four consecutive laps. The decision to show this flag rests solely with the Stewards of the Meeting, the team concerned will immediately be informed of the decision.

GREEN FLAG
This should be used to indicate that the track is clear and should be waved at the observation post immediately after the incident that necessitated the use of one or more yellow flags.

It may also be used, if deemed necessary by the Clerk of the Course, to signal the start of a warm-up lap or the start of a practice session.

WHITE FLAG
This flag should be waved and is used to indicate to the driver that there is a much slower vehicle on the sector of track controlled by that flag point.

BLUE FLAG
This should normally be waved, as an indication to a driver that he is about to be overtaken. It has different meanings during practice and the race

At all times: A stationary flag should be displayed to a driver leaving the pits if traffic is approaching on the track.

During practice: Give way to a faster car which is about to overtake you.

During the race: The Flag should normally be shown to a car about to be lapped and, when shown, the driver concerned must allow the following car to pass at the earliest opportunity.

BLACK & WHITE FLAG DEVIDED DIAGONALLY
This flag should be shown once only and is a warning to the driver concerned that he has been reported for unsportsmanlike behaviour.

BLACK FLAG WITH ORANGE CIRCLE
This flag should be used to inform the driver concerned that his car has mechanical problems likely to endanger himself or others and means that the he must stop at his pit on the next lap. When the mechanical problems have been rectified to the satisfaction of the chief scrutineer the car may rejoin the race.

YELLOW FLAG WITH RED STRIPS
This should be shown motionless to inform drivers that there is a deterioration of adhesion due to oil or water on the track in the area beyond the flag.

This flag should be displayed, for at least (depending on the circumstances) 4 laps unless the surface returns to normal beforehand. It is not however necessary for the sector beyond where this flag is being shown to show a green flag.

CHEQUERED FLAG
This flag should be waved to signify the end of a practice session or the race.

SAFETY CAR
When the order is given to deploy the safety car, all marshal posts will display waved yellow flags and a board «SC» which shall be maintained until the intervention is over.

Flag Dimensions:
The minimum size of all flags is 60cm x 80cm except the red and chequered flags which should be at least 80cm x 100cm. Black flag with orange circle, the circle is 40cm in Diameter.

Information Source FIA:
International Sporting Code (06/01/2011).
Appendix H. Chapter 2.9 Safety Car Procedures. Chapter 2.3 Marshal Posts & 2.3.3 Equipment.
Chapter 2.4 Signalling. More information can be found on the FIA website. www.FIA.com

A

Apex - The point at which the ideal racing line touches the inner radius of a corner.

Aquaplaning - It's what happens when there is more water between the tyres and the road than can be displaced by the tyre tread. The car floats on top of the water and consequently cannot be controlled by the driver.

B

Blistering - Formation of blisters on the tyres, caused by excessive use. The negative consequence is reduction in grip.

Brake Discs - The carbon brake discs used in Formula 1 may not be thicker than 28mm and their diameter may not exceed 278mm, when braking, the discs heat up to as much as 1000 degrees Celsius within a single second. Full breaking will bring a Formula 1 car from 200 km/h to 0 km/h to a full stop, with a 55 metre breaking distance, all within 1.9 seconds. Deceleration forces achieve up to 5G's, the driver has to endure five times his own weight.

C

Carbon Fibre - A construction material for Formula 1 cars. The monocoque, for example, is made from epoxy resin reinforced with carbon fibre. These materials, when laminated together, give great rigidity and strength, but are very lightweight.

Chassis - The central part of a Formula 1 car, with the main components being the monocoque, all the components are connected to the strong, lightweight monocoque. These are bonded to aluminium and Nomex® honeycombs to form a sandwich panel shell structure.

Chicanes - Tight corners that race organisers use to break up long, straight streches of a circuit for safty reasons. Chicanes force drivers to reduce their speed.

Crash Barrier - Safety measures at track locations where there are no run-off zones.

D

Diffuser - Air outlet at the rear of the cars under-body that has a strong influence on the aerodynamic properties. Rising to the rear, the tail ensures a controlled air stream on the under body which generates low pressure under the car and supplies the downforce critical to fast cornering.

Downforce - This is what presses Formula 1 cars down onto the ground. It is generated by low pressure conditions under the body of the car as well as by the angle of attack of the front and rear wings, and enhances the grip.

E

Electronic Control Unit (ECU) - The control unit records all electronic processes in the Formula 1.

Electric Blanket - The tyres require an operational temperature of around 100 degrees Celsius to achieve optimal effectiveness. To reach this temperature quickly, special blankets pre heat the tyres to between 60 and 80 degrees Celsius.

Engine - Only four stroke V8 2.4 litre engines may be used in Formula 1. Eight million ignitions occur in a Formula 1 engine over an average race distance of 300km per Grand Prix.

F

Fuel - Super unleaded fuel is used in Formula 1 cars. From 2008 season onwards 5.75% of the fuel must originate from biological sources.

G

Graining - Due to excessive use, tyres show signs of corrosion and the rubber compound begins to disintegrate, this is referred to as graining. The negative consequence is reduction in grip.

Gravel Trap - Secure run-off zone at a racing circuit which quickly slows down cars that have gone off the track.

RACING TERMS

H

Hairpin - A narrow 180 degree bend. The most famous hairpin is the former Loews hairpin in Monaco, which is now known as the Grand Hotel hairpin.

K

Kerbs - Raised kerbstones lining corners or chicanes on racing tracks. The kerbs provide additional safety as the drivers must reduce their speed when driving over them

Kevlar - Highly durable artificial fibre used in the covering of the headrest. Combined to form a composite with epoxy resin, it has high strength, but very lightweight.

L

Lollipop - The signal pole with a sign saying "Gear" on one side and "Brake" on the other side. During pit stop, the chief mechanic posted in front of the car uses the sign to show the driver when he should apply brake and when he should shift gear and drive off.

M

Monocoque - French for single shell. A safety cell made of carbon fibre composite which forms a protective shell around the driver. The driver is surrounded by deformable structures which absorb energy in an accident.

P

Parc Fermé (PF) - Restricted area of the pit lane.

Pit Lane / Stop - This is where changes to the car take place during the race. Since the 2004 season, the speed limit in the pit lane has been raised from 80km/h to 100km/h but will be reduced to 80 km/h again in 2008. During a regular pit stop in a race, a team of 23 mechanics replace the tyres and/or refuels the car.

Points System - Since 2003 to 2009 season, the first eight drivers in each race are awarded points for the championship ranking. The winner of the Grand Prix is awarded 10 points and the runners up receive 8, 6, 5, 4, 3, 2 and 1 respectively. The same points system is used for the constructors championship.

1st = 10 pts · **2nd** = 8 pts · **3rd** = 6 pts · **4th** = 5 pts · **5th** = 4 pts · **6th** = 3 pts · **7th** = 2 pts · **8th** = 1 pt

In 2010 the points system changed for the new 2010 season, which is as follows:

1st = 25 pts · **2nd** = 18 pts · **3rd** = 15 pts · **4th** = 12 pts · **5th** = 10 pts
6th = 8 pts · **7th** = 6 pts · **8th** = 4 pts · **9th** = 2 pts · **10th** = 1 pt

Pole Position - First place in the starting order for the race, which is given to the fastest driver in qualifying. Qualifying take place a day before the main race.

R

Race Stop - If weather conditions are poor enough to endanger safe driving e.g. heavy rain, snow fog etc, or if a car is blocking the track, a red flag signals that the race has been stopped.

Racing Line - The racing line is the imaginary line on which the circuit can be driven in the fastest possible time, due to the rubber build up, this is also usually where the grip is best.

Rear Lights - Decreases the risk of pile-ups. When using wet weather tyres, the rear lights must always be switched on. It consists of 30 individual LEDs. Must be at least six times 6cm in size and is required to be attached 35cm above the car's underside.

Rear Wing - Creates downward pressure mainly upon the rear axle. The rear wing is adapted to the conditions of the circuit. The steeper it is, the more downforce is created.

Refuelling - 2010 season refuelling has been abolished, the cars must now run on one tank of fuel for the entire race. Fuel tanks will need to be significantly larger for the 2010 car, capable of carrying at least 235 litres instead of the 80 litres in the 2009 season, which allowed refuelling.

S

Safety Belt - The safety belt used in the monocoque is known as a six point harness and can be opened with a single hand movement in case of emergencies.

Sidepods - Side cladding to the cockpit which is integrated in the monocoque. The sidepods contain crash structures that absorb the forces arising from an accident or impact. The Formula 1 car's radiator is also located behind these sidepods.

Slicks - These are tyres without tread and where outlawed by the FIA in late 1997. But where reintroduced in 2009.

Slipstream - Low pressure area behind a Formula 1 car created by air currents. Driving in the slipstream can provide a boost to a car's speed, making it the ideal position for an overtaking manoeuvre.

Speed Limiter - The cruise control feature used in the Formula 1 pit lanes. It is activated by pressing a button on the steering wheel. Speed is then reduced down to the limit for the pit lane.

Steering Wheel - The control centre of the racing car. The steering wheel is not just for turning corners, it's screen displays car statistics for the driver and it has a selection of buttons to allow the driver to adjust some of the car's settings.

Super-Licence - A Formula 1 driving licence is issued by the FIA. In the interest of safety, it is only granted on the basis of good results in the junior series or, in exceptional cases, if other proof of ability can be supplied. It may also be granted under provisional terms.

T

Telemetry - A system allowing a large quantity of data, e.g. concerning chassis, engine, tyres etc, to be recorded in the car and transmitted to the pits. There, the data is analysed to determine any faults, like loss of brake fluid or slow punctures. It also give the ability to improve the car's set up.

Time Penalty - This is a penalty during the race for drivers who have violated regulations. Once his team has been informed by the racing commissioners, the driver must drive through the pit lane within the next three laps. He may not stop there to change tyres or refuel. Entering the pit lane costs the penalised driver valuable time.

Traction - This term describes the ability of a race car to apply it's engine's power to the track, without spinning the wheels.

Image Copyright © Holders:
Sauber Motorsport, Mercedes-Benz Grand Prix, Red Bull Racing, Ferrari SpA

ADDITIONAL DRIVER INFORMATION

MARK WEBBER
159 Grand Prix involvements:
2002 · DNS · Minardi AsiaTech · Wing Fault
2005 · DNS · BMW Williams · Withdrew (USA GP)

SEBASTIAN VETTEL
69 Grand Prix involvements:
2006 · BMW Sauber · 3rd Driver (5 Times)
2007 · BMW Sauber · 3rd Driver (2 Times)

JARNO TRULLI
238 Grand Prix involvements:
1997 · DNS · Minardi Hart · Hydraulics
1999 · DNS · Prost Peugeot · Engine
2001 · DSQ · Jordan Honda · Austrian GP
2005 · DNS · Toyota · Withdrew (USA GP)
2010 · DNS · Virgin Cosworth · Hydraulics

ADRIAN SUTIL
74 Grand Prix involvements:
2006 · Midland F1 Toyota · 3rd Diver (2 Times)
2006 · Spyker Ferrari · 3rd Driver (1 Time)

FELIPE MASSA
135 Grand Prix involvements:
2005 · DNS · Sauber Petronas · Withdrew
2009 · DNS · Ferrari · Accident

TIMO GLOCK
70 Grand Prix involvements:
2004 · Jordan Ford · 3rd Driver (14 Times)
2009 · DNS · Toyota · Accident
2010 · DNS · Virgin Cosworth · Engine

JENSON BUTTON
191 Grand Prix involvements:
2003 · DNS · BAR Honda · Accident
2005 · Ban · BAR Honda · Spanish GP
2005 · Ban · BAR Honda · Monaco GP
2005 · DNS · BAR Honda · Withdrew (USA GP)
2005 · DSQ · Jordan Honda · San Marino GP

RUBENS BARRICHELLO
307 Grand Prix involvements:
1994 · DNQ · Jordan Hart · Accident
1998 · Pile up · Stewart Cosworth · Belgian GP
1999 · DSQ · Jordan Honda · Spanish GP
2002 · DNS · Ferrari · Electrics
2002 · DNS · Ferrari · Electronics
2008 · DSQ · Honda · Australian GP

FERNANDO ALONSO
159 Grand Prix involvements:
2005 · DNS · Renault · Withdrew (USA GP)

MICHAEL SCHUMACHER
269 Grand Prix involvements:
1994 · DSQ · Benetton Ford · British GP
1994 · DSQ · Benetton Ford · Belgian GP
1994 · Ban · Benetton Ford · Italian GP
1994 · Ban · Benetton Ford · Portuguese GP
1996 · DNS · Ferrari · Engine

VITANTONIO LIUZZI
76 Grand Prix involvements:
2005 · Red Bull Cosworth · 3rd Driver (13 Times)

KAMUI KOBAYASHI
22 Grand Prix involvements:
2009 · Toyota · 3rd Driver (1 Time)

ROBERT KUBICA
88 Grand Prix involvements:
2006 · BMW Sauber · 3rd Driver (12 Times)

The additional Driver information is provided to clarify the difference between Grand Prix Starts and Grand Prix Involvements. DNQ's, DSQ's & Race Bans are not included.

Example: MARK WEBBER

Grand Prix Starts: 157
Grand Prix Involvements: 159

Of the 159 involvements, there were 2 incidents where he didn't race, as a result the number of starts would be 157:

1. 2002 Minardi AsiaTech withdrew from the Spanish GP due to front wing failure.

2. 2005 BMW Williams withdrew from the USA GP due to tyre problems with Michelin.

LOTUS RENAULT GP

ROBERT KUBICA - 2011

Date of Birth	7th December 1984
Place of Birth	Krakow, Poland
Nationality	Polish
Web Site	www.kubica.pl

GRAND PRIX STATISTICS	
First Grand Prix: Hungarian GP 2006	
GP Starts: 76	Wins: 1
Pole Positions: 1	Fastest Laps: 1
Podiums: 12	Total Points: 273
2010 Position: 8th	2010 Points: 136

GRAND PRIX HISTORY

2010	Renault • 136 Pts • 8th
2009	BMW Sauber • 17 Pts • 14th
2008	BMW Sauber • 75 Pts • 4th
2007	BMW Sauber • 39 Pts • 6th
2006	BMW Sauber • 6 Pts • 16th

BAHRAIN GRAND PRIX - SAKHIR (MANAMA)

Circuit Name : Bahrain International Circuit			
No of Laps: **Total Distance:**	57 308.238 km · 191.530 miles	**Lap Record:** **F1 Car:**	Michael Schumacher Ferrari F2004
Circuit Length:	5.412 km · 3.363 miles	**Time · Date:**	1:30.252 · 04/04/2004
Web Site:	www.bahraingp.com.bh	**Lap Speed:** **(average)**	216.061 km/h 134.262 mph
Address:	Bahrain International Circuit, P.O. Box 26381, Manama, Kingdom of Bahrain Telephone : +973 1745 0000 · Fax : +973 1745 1111		

Winners @ Bahrain International Circuit

Year · Driver · Constructor	Year · Driver · Constructor
2010 · Fernando Alonso · Ferrari 2009 · Jenson Button · Brawn-Mercedes 2008 · Felipe Massa · Ferrari 2007 · Felipe Massa · Ferrari 2006 · Fernando Alonso · Renault 2005 · Fernando Alonso · Renault 2004 · Michael Schumacher · Ferrari	

The **2011 Bahrain Grand Prix** was scheduled to be the opening round for the 2011 Formula 1 season. Planned to be held on 13 March 2011 at the Bahrain International Circuit in Sakhir, Bahrain, it was postponed on 21 February 2011 due to local civil unrest.

An FIA statement read: "The World Motor Sport Council asked the Bahrain Motor Federation to communicate by 1 May 2011 at the latest if the Bahrain Grand Prix can be organised in 2011."

Team Winners:	Brawn GP 1 · Ferrari 4 · Renault 2

Circuit Name : Bahrain International Circuit			
Time Zone	GMT +3	**Top Speed**	~315 km/h • ~196 mph
Circuit Direction	Clockwise	**Latitude**	26° 1' 57" N
Capacity	94,000 ±	**Longitude**	50° 30' 38" E
Turns	15	**Years GP Held**	7

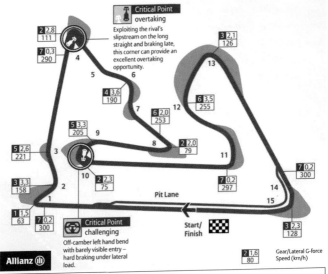

Critical Point
overtaking
Exploiting the rival's slipstream on the long straight and braking late, this corner can provide an excellent overtaking opportunity.

Critical Point
challenging
Off-camber left hand bend with barely visible entry – hard braking under lateral load.

Pit Lane

Start/Finish

Gear/Lateral G-force
Speed (km/h)

Allianz (Ⓡ)

2010 Circuit Results : Bahrain International Circuit

Position • Driver • Team/Engine • Time/Gap • Speed

Pole Position • Sebastian Vettel • Red Bull-Renault • 1m 54.101s • 198.740 km/h
Fastest Lap • Fernando Alonso • Ferrari • 1m 58.287s • 191.706 km/h • On Lap 45

1st • Fernando Alonso • Ferrari • 1h 39m 20.396s • 186.272 km/h
2nd • Felipe Massa • Ferrari • +16.099s • 185.770 km/h
3rd • Lewis Hamilton • McLaren-Mercedes • +23.182s • 185.550 km/h

Notes:

FOLLOW THEM . . . .

HTTP www.redbullracing.com

www.twitter.com/redbullf1spy

www.facebook.com/redbullracing

You Tube www.youtube.com/mko90nji

Sebastian Vettel - www.sebastianvettel.de

Mark Webber - www.markwebber.com

www.twitter.com/aussiegrit

www.facebook.com/pages/Mark-Webber/11916742586

VODAFONE McLAREN MERCEDES

HTTP www.mclaren.com

www.twitter.com/thefifthdriver

www.facebook.com/vodafonemclarenmercedes

Lewis Hamilton - www.lewishamilton.com

www.twitter.com/IamLewis4real

Jenson Button - www.jensonbutton.com

www.twitter.com/JensonButton

www.facebook.com/pages/Jenson-Button/10635878202

Notes:

HTTP www.ferrari.com/English/Formula1/Pages/Home.aspx

www.twitter.com/insideferrari

www.facebook.com/Ferrari#!/pages/SF-Scuderia-Ferrari/59567929391

You Tube www.youtube.com/user/ferrariworld

Fernando Alonso - www.fernandoalonso.com/en

Felipe Massa - www.felipemassa.com

HTTP www.mercedes-gp.com

www.twitter.com/OfficialMGP

www.facebook.com/MERCEDESGPPETRONAS

You Tube www.youtube.com/user/MercedesGPPetronas

Michael Schumacher - www.michael-schumacher.de

Nico Rosberg - www.nicorosberg.com

www.twitter.com/nico_rosberg

www.facebook.com/nicorosberg

Notes:

FOLLOW THEM . . . .

www.lotusrenaultgp.com

www.twitter.com/OfficialLRGP

www.facebook.com/pages/Lotus-Renault-GP-The-Official/173854285966083

Nick Heidfeld - www.nickheidfeld.com

www.twitter.com/nickheidfeld

Petrov Vitaly - www.vitalypetrov.ru/en

www.twitter.com/vitalypetrov10

www.facebook.com/pages/Vitaly-Petrovru/154513514597652

www.youtube.com/user/vitalypetrovru

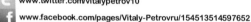

www.williamsf1.com

www.twitter.com/williamsf1team

www.facebook.com/pages/Williams-F1/339720108887

Rubens Barrichello - www.barrichello.com.br

www.twitter.com/rubarrichello

Pastor Maldonado - www.pastormaldonado.com/

www.twitter.com/Pastormaldo

Notes:

HTTP www.forceindiaf1.com

www.twitter.com/clubforce

www.facebook.com/forceindiaf1

You Tube www.youtube.com/user/forceindiaformulaone

Adrian Sutil - www.adrian-sutil.de

Paul di Resta - www.pauldiresta.com

www.twitter.com/pauldirestaf1

www.facebook.com/pages/Paul-Di-Resta/140487912647176

 Sauber F1 Team

HTTP www.sauberf1team.com

www.twitter.com/OfficialSF1Team

www.facebook.com/sauberf1team

Kamui Kobayashi - www.kamui-kobayashi.com

Sergio Pérez - www.sergioperezf1.com/en/

www.twitter.com/checoperez17

www.facebook.com/pages/Sergio-Perez/128555773042

●● www.flickr.com/photos/sergioperezf1

You Tube www.youtube.com/sergioperezf1

Notes:

HTTP www.tororosso.com

www.twitter.com/tororossospy

www.facebook.com/tororosso

Sébastien Buemi - www.buemi.ch

www.twitter.com/sebastien_buemi

www.facebook.com/group.php?gid=61465089890

You Tube www.youtube.com/sebuemi

Jaime Alguersuari - www.jalguersuari.com

www.twitter.com/jalguersuaricom

www.facebook.com/pages/Jaime-Alguersuari-Official-Fan-Club/111384065572293

HTTP www.teamlotus.co.uk

www.twitter.com/myteamlotus

www.facebook.com/TeamLotus

●● www.flickr.com/photos/myteamlotus

Jarno Trulli - www.jarnotrulli.com

Heikki Kovalainen - www.heikkikovalainen.com

www.twitter.com/H_Kovalainen

www.facebook.com/Heikki.Kovalainen.Official.Fan.Page

●● www.flickr.com/photos/officialkovalainen/sets

You Tube www.youtube.com/officialkovalainen

FOLLOW THEM ....

 HISPANIA RACING

 www.hispaniaf1team.com

www.twitter.com/HispaniaRacing

Narain Karthikeyan - www.narainracing.com

www.twitter.com/NarainRacing

Vitantonio Liuzzi - www.liuzzi.com

www.twitter.com/_____

 |

MARUSSIA **VIRGIN RACING**

 www.marussiavirginracing.com

www.twitter.com/MarussiaVirgin

www.facebook.com/VirginRacingF1

Timo Glock - www.timoglock.de

www.twitter.com/realTimoGlock

www.facebook.com/TimoGlockofficial

Jérôme d'Ambrosio - www.jeromedambrosio.com

 PIRELLI

 www.pirelli.com/tyre/ww/en/motorsport-world/genericPage/formula_1

www.twitter.com/pirelli_media

 www.facebook.com/Pirelli

●● www.flickr.com/photos/pirelli/sets

You Tube www.youtube.com/pirelli

RESULTS TABLES

DRIVERS CHAMPIONSHIP FILL-IN CHART 2011

CONSTRUCTORS & DRIVERS 2010 RESULTS

CONSTRUCTORS & DRIVERS 2009 RESULTS

World Champions

Drivers
1950 - 2010

Constructors
1958 - 2010

Bloodhound
Supersonic Car

Racing Notes

Autograph Pages

Imaging by Hywel Vaughan

BLOODHOUND SSC modelled in full

SIEMENS

2011 - DRIVER FILL-IN CHART

F1 DRIVERS	NAT	AUS 27 Mar	MYS 10 Apr	CHN 17 Apr	TUR 8 May	ESP 22 May	MCO 29 May	CAN 12 Jun	EUR 26 Jun	GBR 10 Jul
1. S Vettel										
2. M Webber										
3. L Hamilton										
4. J Button										
5. F Alonso										
6. F Massa										
7. M Schumacher										
8. N Rosberg										
9. N Heidfeld										
10. V Petrov										
11. R Barrichello										
12. P Maldonado										
14. A Sutil										
15. P di Resta										
16. K Kobayashi										
17. S Pérez										
18. S Buemi										
19. J Alguersuari										
20. H Kovalainen										
21. J Trulli										
22. N Karthikeyan										
23. V Liuzzi										
24. T Glock										
25. J d'Ambrosio										
26.										
27.										
R. Kubica										

1st = 25pts · 2nd = 18pts · 3rd = 15pts · 4th = 12pts · 5th = 10pts · 6th = 8pts · 7th = 6pts · 8th = 4pts · 9th = 2pts · 10th = 1pt
DNF = Did Not Finish · DNS = Did Not Start · DSQ = Disqualified · DNQ = Did Not Qualify · P = Pole Position · F = Fastest Lap

2011 - DRIVER FILL-IN CHART

DEU 24 Jul	HUN 31 Jul	BEL 28 Aug	ITA 11 Sep	SGP 25 Sep	JPN 9 Oct	KOR 16 Oct	IND 30 Oct	UAE 13 Nov	BRA 27 Nov	BHR N/A	Total Points

1st = 25pts • 2nd = 18pts • 3rd = 15pts • 4th = 12pts • 5th = 10pts • 6th = 8pts • 7th = 6pts • 8th = 4pts • 9th = 2pts • 10th = 1pt
DNF = Did Not Finish • DNS = Did Not Start • DSQ = Disqualified • DNQ = Did Not Qualify • P = Pole Position • F = Fastest Lap

2010 - CONSTRUCTOR RESULTS TABLE

TEAM ENGINE · CHASSIS		BHR 14/3	AUS 28/3	MYS 4/4	CHN 18/4	ESP 9/5	MCO 16/5	TUR 30/5	CAN 13/6
1. Red Bull Racing Renault RS27-2010 · RB6		16	2	43	12	40	43	15	22
2. Vodafone McLaren Mercedes FO 108X · MP4-25		21	33	12	43	10	10	43	43
3. Scuderia Ferrari Ferrari 056 · F10		43	27	6	14	26	20	10	15
4. Mercedes GP Mercedes FO 108X · MGP W01		18	11	15	16	12	6	22	8
5. Renault F1 Team Renault RS27-2010 · R30		0	18	12	16	4	15	8	6
6. AT&T Williams Cosworth CA2010 · FW32		1	4	1	0	2	0	0	0
7. Force India F1 Team Mercedes FO 108X · VJM03		2	6	10	0	6	6	2	3
8. BMW Sauber F1 Team Ferrari 056 · C29		0	0	0	0	0	0	1	0
9. Scuderia Toro Rosso Ferrari 056 · STR5		0	0	2	0	1	1	0	4
10. Lotus Racing Cosworth CA2010 · T127		0	0	0	0	0	0	0	0
11. HRT F1 Team Cosworth CA2010 · F110		0	0	0	0	0	0	0	0
12. Virgin Racing Cosworth CA2010 · VR-01		0	0	0	0	0	0	0	0

RED BULL RACING - F1 2010 CONSTRUCTORS CHAMPION - 498 POINTS

Image Copyright © Red Bull Racing

2010 - CONSTRUCTOR RESULTS TABLE

EUR 27/6	GBR 11/7	DEU 25/7	HUN 1/8	BEL 29/8	ITA 12/9	SGP 26/9	JPN 10/10	KOR 24/10	BRA 7/11	UAE 14/11	Total Points
25	31	23	40	18	20	33	40	0	43	29	498
33	30	22	4	25	18	12	22	18	22	33	454
4	0	43	30	12	40	29	15	40	15	7	396
1	17	6	0	14	12	10	8	12	14	12	214
10	0	7	10	17	4	6	0	10	2	18	163
12	11	0	9	0	7	9	2	7	4	0	69
8	4	0	0	11	0	2	0	8	0	0	68
6	8	0	8	4	0	0	10	6	1	0	44
2	0	0	0	0	0	0	1	0	0	2	13
0	0	0	0	0	0	0	0	0	0	0	0
0	0	0	0	0	0	0	0	0	0	0	0
0	0	0	0	0	0	0	0	0	0	0	0

SEBASTIAN VETTEL - F1 2010 WORLD CHAMPION - 256 POINTS

2010 - DRIVER RESULTS TABLE

F1 DRIVERS	NAT	BHR 14 Mar	AUS 28 Mar	MYS 4 Apr	CHN 18 Apr	ESP 9 May	MCO 16 May	TUR 30 May	CAN 13 Jun
1. S Vettel		4 P / 12	DNF P / ME	1 / 25	6 P / 8	3 / 15	2 F / 18	DNF / AC	4 / 12
2. F Alonso		1 F / 25	4 / 12	13	4 / 12	2 / 18	6 / 8	8 / 4	3 / 15
3. M Webber		8 / 4	9 F / 2	2 P F / 18	8 / 4	1 P / 25	1 P / 25	3 P / 15	5 / 10
4. L Hamilton		3 / 15	6 / 8	6 / 8	2 F / 18	14 F	5 / 10	1 / 25	1 P / 25
5. J Button		7 / 6	1 / 25	8 / 4	1 / 25	5 / 10	DNF / EN	2 / 18	2 / 18
6. F Massa		2 / 18	3 / 15	7 / 6	9 / 2	6 / 8	4 / 12	7 / 6	15
7. N Rosberg		5 / 10	5 / 10	3 / 15	3 / 15	13	7 / 6	5 / 10	6 / 8
8. R Kubica		11	2 / 18	4 / 12	5 / 10	8 / 4	3 / 15	6 / 8	7 F / 6
9. M Schumacher		6 / 8	10 / 1	DNF / ME	10 / 1	4 / 12	12	4 / 12	11
10. R Barrichello		10 / 1	8 / 4	12	12	9 / 2	DNF / AC	14	14
11. A Sutil		12	DNF / EN	5 / 10	11	7 / 6	8 / 4	9 / 2	10 / 1
12. K Kobayashi		DNF / EN	DNF / AC	DNF / EN	DNF / AC	12	DNF / ME	10 / 1	DNF / AC
13. V Petrov		DNF / ME	DNF / SP	DNF / ME	7 / 6	11	13	15 F	17
14. N Hülkenberg		14	DNF / AC	10 / 1	15	16	DNF / AC	17	13
15. V Liuzzi		9 / 2	7 / 6	DNF / ME	DNF / AC	ME	9 / 2	13	9 / 2
16. S Buemi		16	DNF / AC	11	DNF / AC	DNF / ME	10 / 1	16	8 / 4
17. P de la Rosa		DNF / EN	12	DNS	DNF / ME	DNF / ME	DNF / ME	11	DNF / EN
18. N Heidfeld		-	-	-	-	-	-	-	-
19. J Alguersuari		13	11	9 / 2	13	10 / 1	11	12	12
20. H Kovalainen		15	13	DNF / ME	14	DNS	DNF / ME	DNF / ME	16
21. J Trulli		17	DNS	17	DNF / ME	17	15	DNF / ME	DNF / ME
22. K Chandhok		DNF / AC	14	15	17	DNF / ME	14	20	18
23. B Senna		DNF / ME	DNF / ME	16	16	DNF / AC	DNF / ME	DNF / ME	DNF / ME
24. L di Grassi		DNF / EN	DNF / ME	14	DNF / ME	19	DNF / ME	19	19
25. T Glock		DNF / ME	DNF / ME	DNF / SP	DNS	18	DNF / ME	18	DNF / ME
26. S Yamamoto		-	-	-	-	-	-	-	-
27. C Klien		-	-	-	-	-	-	-	-

DNF = Did Not Finish • DNS = Did Not Start • DSQ = Disqualified • P = Pole Position • F = Fastest Lap
ME = Mechanical • SP = Spin • EN = Engine • AC = Accident • *Italics Numbers = Points* • Black Numbers = Position

2010 - DRIVER RESULTS TABLE

EUR 27 Jun	GBR 11 Jul	DEU 25 Jul	HUN 1 Aug	BEL 29 Aug	ITA 12 Sep	SGP 26 Sep	JPN 10 Oct	KOR 24 Oct	BRA 7 Nov	UAE 14 Nov	Total PTS
1 P *25*	7 P *6*	3 P F *15*	3 P F *15*	15	4 *12*	2 *18*	1 P *25*	DNF P EN	1 *25*	1 P *25*	256
8 *4*	14 F	1 *25*	2 *18*	DNF AC	1 P F *25*	1 P F *25*	3 *15*	1 F *25*	3 *15*	7 *6*	252
DNF AC	1 *25*	6	1 *25*	2 P *18*	6 *8*	3 *15*	2 F *18*	DNF AC	2 *18*	8 *4*	242
2 *18*	2 *18*	4 *12*	DNF MH	1 F *25*	DNF AC	DNF AC	5 *10*	2 *18*	4 F *12*	2 F *18*	240
3 F *15*	4 *12*	5 *10*	8 *4*	DNF AC	2 *18*	4 *12*	4 *12*	12	5 *10*	3 *15*	214
11	15	2 *18*	4 *12*	4 *12*	3 *15*	8 *4*	DNF AC	3 *15*	15	10 *1*	144
10 *1*	3 *15*	8 *4*	DNF MH	6 *8*	5 *10*	5 *10*	17	DNF AC	6 *8*	4 *12*	142
5 *10*	DNF MH	7 *6*	DNF AC	3 *15*	8 *4*	7 *6*	DNF MH	5 *10*	9 *2*	5 *10*	136
15	9 *2*	9 *2*	11	7 *6*	9 *2*	13	6 *8*	4 *12*	7 *6*	DNF AC	72
4 *12*	5 *10*	12	10 *1*	DNF AC	10 *1*	6 *8*	9 *2*	7 *6*	14	12	47
6 *8*	8 *4*	17	DNF AC	5 *10*	16	9 *2*	DNF MH	DNF AC	12	13	47
7 *6*	6 *8*	11	9 *2*	8 *4*	DNF MH	DNF AC	7 *6*	8 *4*	10 *1*	14	32
14	13	10 *1*	5 *10*	9 *2*	13	11	DNF AC	DNF AC	16	6 *8*	27
DNF MH	10 *1*	13	6 *8*	14	7 *6*	10 *1*	DNF AC	10 *1*	8 P *4*	16	22
16	11	16	13	10 *1*	12	DNF AC	DNF AC	6 *8*	DNF AC	DNF AC	21
9 *2*	12	DNF AC	12	12	11	14	10 *1*	DNF AC	13	15	8
12	DNF AC	14	7 *6*	11	14	-	-	-	-	-	6
-	-	-	-	-	--	DNF AC	8 *4*	9 *2*	17	11	6
13	DNF MH	15	DNF MH	13	15	12	11	11	11	9 *2*	5
DNF AC	17	DNF AC	14	16	18	16	12	13	18	17	0
21	16	DNF MH	15	19	DNF MH	DNF MH	13	DNF MH	19	21	0
18	19	-	-	-	-	-	-	-	-	-	0
20	-	19	17	DNF MH	DNF MH	DNF AC	15	14	21	19	0
17	DNF MH	DNF MH	18	17	20	15	DNS	DNF AC	DNF AC	18	0
19	18	18	16	18	17	DNF MH	14	DNF AC	20	DNF MH	0
-	20	DNF MH	19	20	19	-	16	15	-	-	0
-	-	-	-	-	-	DNF AC	-	-	22	20	0

DNF = Did Not Finish · DNS = Did Not Start · DSQ = Disqualified · P = Pole Position · F = Fastest Lap
ME = Mechanical · SP = Spin · EN = Engine · AC = Accident · *Italics Numbers = Points* · Black Numbers = Position

2009 - CONSTRUCTOR RESULTS TABLE

TEAM ENGINE · CHASSIS	NAT	AUS 29 Mar	MYS 5 Apr	CHN 19 Apr	BHR 26 Apr	ESP 10 May	MCO 24 May
1. Brawn GP Mercedes FO 108W · BGP001		18	7	11	14	18	18
2. Red Bull Racing Renault RS27-2009 · RB5		0	1.5	18	8	11	4
3. Vodafone McLaren Mercedes Mercedes FO 108W · MP4-24		0	1	7	5	0	0
4. Scuderia Ferrari Marlboro Ferrari 056 · F60		0	0	0	3	3	11
5. Panasonic Toyota Racing Toyota RVX-09 · TF109		11	5.5	2	8	0	0
6. BMW Sauber F1 Team BMW P86/09 · F1.09		0	4	0	0	2	0
7. AT&T Williams Toyota RVX-09 · FW31		3	0.5	0	0	1	3
8. Renault F1 Team Renault RS27-2009 · R29		4	0	0	1	4	2
9. Force India F1 Team Mercedes FO 108W · VJM02		0	0	0	0	0	0
10. Scuderia Toro Rosso Ferrari 056 · STR4		3	0	1	0	0	1

BRAWN GP - F1 2009 CONSTRUCTORS CHAMPION - 172 POINTS

TUR 7 Jun	GBR 21 Jun	DEU 19 Jul	HUN 26 Jul	EUR 23 Aug	BEL 30 Aug	ITA 13 Sep	SGP 27 Sep	JPN 4 Oct	BRA 18 Oct	UAE 1 Nov	Total PTS
10	9	7	2	12	2	18	7	3	5	11	172
14	18	18	6	0	6	1	5	10	15	18	153.5
0	0	1	14	13	3	3	12	6	6	0	71
3	6	6	8	6	10	6	0	5	3	0	70
6	2	0	4	0	0	0	8	8	0	5	59.5
2	0	0	0	1	9	2	1	3	8	4	36
4	4	5	5	4	1	0	0	4	0	0	34.5
0	0	2	0	3	0	4	6	0	0	0	26
0	0	0	0	0	8	5	0	0	0	0	13
0	0	0	0	0	0	0	0	0	2	1	8

JENSON BUTTON - F1 2009 WORLD CHAMPION - 95 POINTS

2009 - DRIVER RESULTS TABLE

F1 DRIVERS	NAT	AUS 29 Mar	MYS* 5 Apr	CHN 19 Apr	BHR 26 Apr	ESP 10 May	MCO 24 May	TUR 7 Jun
1. J Button		1 P *10*	1 P F *5*	3 *6*	1 *10*	1 P *10*	1 P *10*	1 F *10*
2. S Vettel		13	15	1 P *10*	2 *8*	4 *5*	DNF	3 P *6*
3. R Barrichello		2 *8*	5 *2*	4 F *5*	5 *4*	2 F *8*	2 *8*	DNF
4. M Webber		12	6 *1.5*	2 *8*	11	3 *6*	5 *4*	2 *8*
5. L Hamilton		4 DSQ	7 *1*	6 *3*	4 *5*	9	12	13
6. K Räikkönen		15	14	10	6 *3*	DNF	3 *6*	9
7. N Rosberg		6 F *3*	8 *0.5*	15	9	8 *1*	6 *3*	5 *4*
8. J Trulli		3 *6*	4 *2.5*	DNF	3 P F *6*	DNF	13	4 *5*
9. F Alonso		5 *4*	11	9	8 *1*	5 *4*	7 *2*	10
10. T Glock		4 *5*	3 *3*	7 *2*	7 *2*	10	10	8 *1*
11. F Massa		DNF	9	DNF	14	6 *3*	4 F *5*	6 *3*
12. H Kovalainen		DNF	DNF	5 *4*	12	DNF	DNF	14
13. N Heidfeld		10	2 *4*	12	19	7 *2*	11	11
14. R Kubica		14	DNF	13	18	11	DNF	7 *2*
15. G Fisichella		11	18	14	15	14	9	DNF
16. S Buemi		7 *2*	16	8 *1*	17	DNF	DNF	15
17. A Sutil		9	17	17	16	DNF	14	17
18. K Kobayashi		-	-	-	-	-	-	-
19. S Bourdais		8 *1*	10	11	13	DNF	8 *1*	18
20. K Nakajima		DNF	12	DNF	DNF	13	15	12
21. N Piquet Jr.		DNF	13	16	10	12	DNF	16
22. V Liuzzi		-	-	-	-	-	-	-
23. R Grosjean		-	-	-	-	-	-	-
24. J Alguersuari		-	-	-	-	-	-	-
25. L Badoer		-	-	-	-	-	-	-

DNF = Did Not Finish · DNS = Did Not Start · DSQ = Disqualified · P = Pole Position · F = Fastest Lap

(F) = Giancarlo Fisichella drove for Ferrari for the last five races of the season.
* Half points were awarded as less than 75% of the scheduled distance was completed.

126

2009 - DRIVER RESULTS TABLE

GBR 21 Jun	DEU 19 Jul	HUN 26 Jul	EUR 23 Aug	BEL 30 Aug	ITA 13 Sep	SGP 27 Sep	JPN 4 Oct	BRA 18 Oct	UAE 1 Nov	Total Points
6 *3*	5 *4*	7 *2*	7 *2*	DNF	2 *8*	5 *4*	8 *1*	5 *4*	3 *6*	95
1 P F *10*	2 *8*	DNF	DNF	3 F *6*	8 *1*	4 *5*	1 P *10*	4 *5*	1 F *10*	84
3 *6*	6 *3*	10	1 *10*	7 *2*	1 *10*	6 *3*	7 *2*	8 P *1*	4 *5*	77
2 *8*	1 P *10*	3 F *6*	9	9	DNF	DNF	17 F	1 F *10*	2 *8*	69.5
16	18	1 *10*	2 P *8*	DNF	12 P	1 P *10*	3 *6*	3 *6*	DNF P	49
8 *1*	DNF	2 *8*	3 *6*	1 *10*	3 *6*	10	4 *5*	6 *3*	12	48
5 *4*	4 *5*	4 *5*	5 *4*	8 *1*	16	11	5 *4*	DNF	9	34.5
7 *2*	17	8 *1*	13	DNF	14	12	2 *8*	DNF	7 *2*	32.5
14	7 F *2*	DNF P	6 *3*	DNF	5 *4*	3 F *6*	10	DNF	14	26
9	9	6 *3*	14 F	10	11	2 *8*	DNS	-	-	24
4 *5*	3 *6*	DNS	-	-	-	-	-	-	-	22
DNF	8 *1*	5 *4*	4 *5*	6 *3*	6 *3*	7 *2*	11	12	11	22
15	10	11	11	5 *4*	7 *2*	DNF	6 *3*	DNF	5 *4*	19
13	14	13	8 *1*	4 *5*	DNF	8 *1*	9	2 *8*	10	17
10	11	14	12	2 P *8*	9 (F)	13 (F)	12 (F)	10 (F)	16 (F)	8
18	16	16	DNF	12	13	DNF	DNF	7 *2*	8 *1*	6
17	15	DNF	10	11	4 F *5*	DNF	13	DNF	17	5
-	-	-	-	-	-	-	-	9	6 *3*	3
DNF	DNF	-	-	-	-	-	-	-	-	2
11	12	9	18	13	10	9	15	DNF	13	0
12	13	12	-	-	-	-	-	-	-	0
-	-	-	-	-	DNF	14	14	11	15	0
-	-	-	15	DNF	15	DNF	16	13	18	0
-	-	15	16	DNF	DNF	DNF	DNF	14	DNF	0
-	-	-	17	14	-	-	-	-	-	0

1st=10pts · 2nd=8pts · 3rd=6pts · 4th=5pts · 5th=4pts · 6th=3pts · 7th=2pts · 8th=1pt
Italics Numbers = Points · Black Numbers = Position

WORLD CHAMPION DRIVERS - 1950 TO 2010

Year	Driver	Team / Engine	Nat	Year	Driver	Team / Engine	Nat
2010	S Vettel	Red Bull-Renault		1979	J Scheckter *	Ferrari	
2009	J Button	Brawn-Mercedes		1978	M Andretti	Lotus-Ford	
2008	L Hamilton	McLaren-Mercedes		1977	N Lauda	Ferrari	
2007	K Räikkönen	Ferrari		1976	J Hunt	McLaren-Ford	
2006	F Alonso	Renault		1975	N Lauda	Ferrari	
2005	F Alonso	Renault		1974	E Fittipaldi	McLaren-Ford	
2004	M Schumacher	Ferrari		1973	J Stewart	Tyrrell-Ford	
2003	M Schumacher	Ferrari		1972	E Fittipaldi	Lotus-Ford	
2002	M Schumacher	Ferrari		1971	J Stewart	Tyrrell-Ford	
2001	M Schumacher	Ferrari		1970	J Rindt	Lotus-Ford	
2000	M Schumacher	Ferrari		1969	J Stewart	Matra-Ford	
1999	M Häkkinen	McLaren-Mercedes		1968	G Hill	Lotus-Ford	
1998	M Häkkinen	McLaren-Mercedes		1967	D Hulme	Brabham-Repco	
1997	J Villeneuve	Williams-Renault		1966	J Brabham	Brabham-Repco	
1996	D Hill	Williams-Renault		1965	J Clark	Lotus-Climax	
1995	M Schumacher	Benetton-Renault		1964	J Surtees	Ferrari	
1994	M Schumacher	Benetton-Ford		1963	J Clark	Lotus-Climax	
1993	A Prost	Williams-Renault		1962	G Hill	BRM	
1992	N Mansell	Williams-Renault		1961	P Hill	Ferrari	
1991	A Senna	McLaren-Honda		1960	J Brabham	Cooper-Climax	
1990	A Senna	McLaren-Honda		1959	J Brabham	Cooper-Climax	
1989	A Prost	McLaren-Honda		1958	M Hawthorn	Ferrari	
1988	A Senna	McLaren-Honda		1957	J M Fangio	Maserati	
1987	N Piquet	Williams Honda		1956	J M Fangio	Ferrari	
1986	A Prost	McLaren-TAG		1955	J M Fangio	Mercedes-Benz	
1985	A Prost	McLaren-TAG		1954	J M Fangio	Maserati/Mercedes	
1984	N Lauda	McLaren-TAG		1953	A Ascari	Ferrari	
1983	N Piquet	Brabham-BMW		1952	A Ascari	Ferrari	
1982	K Rosberg	Williams-Ford		1951	J M Fangio	Alfa Romeo	
1981	N Piquet	Brabham-Ford		1950	G Farina	Alfa Romeo	
1980	A Jones	Williams-Ford					

Note: Drivers Championship started in 1950. | * South Africa changed Flag on 27th April 1994.

Year	Constructor / Points	Tyre Used	Nat	Year	Constructor / Points	Tyre Used	Nat
2010	Red Bull-Renault · 498	Bridgestone		1979	Ferrari · 113	Michelin	
2009	Brawn-Mercedes · 172	Bridgestone		1978	Lotus-Ford · 86	Goodyear	
2008	Ferrari · 172	Bridgestone		1977	Ferrari · 95	Goodyear	
2007	Ferrari · 204	Bridgestone		1976	Ferrari · 83	Goodyear	
2006	Renault · 206	Michelin		1975	Ferrari · 72.5	Goodyear	
2005	Renault · 191	Michelin		1974	McLaren-Ford · 73	Goodyear	
2004	Ferrari · 262	Bridgestone		1973	Lotus-Ford · 92	Goodyear	
2003	Ferrari · 158	Bridgestone		1972	Lotus-Ford · 61	Firestone	
2002	Ferrari · 221	Bridgestone		1971	Tyrrell-Ford · 73	Goodyear	
2001	Ferrari · 179	Bridgestone		1970	Lotus-Ford · 59	Firestone	
2000	Ferrari · 170	Bridgestone		1969	Matra-Ford · 66	Dunlop	
1999	Ferrari · 128	Bridgestone		1968	Lotus-Ford · 62	Firestone	
1998	McLaren · 156	Bridgestone		1967	Brabham-Repco · 63	Goodyear	
1997	Williams-Renault · 123	Goodyear		1966	Brabham-Repco · 42	Goodyear	
1996	Williams-Renault · 175	Goodyear		1965	Lotus-Climax · 54	Dunlop	
1995	Benetton-Renault · 137	Goodyear		1964	Ferrari · 45	Dunlop	
1994	Williams-Renault · 118	Goodyear		1963	Lotus-Climax · 54	Dunlop	
1993	Williams-Renault · 168	Goodyear		1962	BRM · 42	Dunlop	
1992	Williams-Renault · 164	Goodyear		1961	Ferrari · 45	Dunlop	
1991	McLaren-Honda · 139	Goodyear		1960	Cooper-Climax · 48	Dunlop	
1990	McLaren-Honda · 121	Goodyear		1959	Cooper-Climax · 40	Dunlop	
1989	McLaren-Honda · 141	Goodyear		1958	Vanwall · 48	Dunlop	
1988	McLaren-Honda · 199	Goodyear					
1987	Williams-Honda · 137	Goodyear					
1986	Williams-Honda · 141	Goodyear					
1985	McLaren-TAG · 90	Goodyear					
1984	McLaren-TAG · 143.5	Michelin					
1983	Ferrari · 89	Goodyear					
1982	Ferrari · 74	Goodyear					
1981	Williams-Ford · 95	Goodyear					
1980	Williams-Ford · 120	Goodyear					

Note: Constructors Championship started in 1958.

WWW.BLOODHOUNDSSC.COM

WORLD LAND SPEED RECORD ATTEMPT

BLOODHOUND SSC
Inspiring the next generation

The BLOODHOUND Project is Britain's latest attempt on the World Land Speed Record with a car capable of 1,000 mph.

Their Mission? To inspire future generations to pursue science, technology, engineering & mathematics by showcasing these subjects in the most exciting way possible in schools, colleges & universities. Richard Noble (Project Director) & Andy Green (Driver) head the team for this exciting endeavour.

These two trailblazers set the current record (763.035 mph) in 1997 with ThustSSC & will attempt to beat their record with BLOODHOUND SSC (SuperSonic Car)

This project is entirely funded by sponsorship from individuals and corporate organisations.

The 1K club is the official BLOODHOUND SSC supporters club, giving you access to members day events, with a chance to meet the team & find out the latest on the project.

Register your school on the website or get involved by going to:

WWW.BLOODHOUNDSSC.COM

Be part of the adventure - join the 1K CLUB

BLOODHOUND SSC ®

BLOODHOUND SSC

The BLOODHOUND SSC (SuperSonic Car) will go from 0 - 1,000 mph in 42 seconds and 0 - 1,000 - 0 mph in 90 seconds. At 1,000 mph the BLOODHOUND is travelling one mile every 3.6 seconds or four and a half football pitches in the blink of an eye. That is 150 metres in one blink. At 1,000 mph BLOODHOUNDs wheels will be turning 10,300 rpm and producing 50,000 lbs of radial 'g' at the rim.

BLOODHOUND SSC STATISTICS

DIMENSIONS
Length	13.4 m
Max Height	2.8m
Wheels (diameter)	0.9 m
Turning Radius	120 m
Car Mass	6422 kg

SPEED & POWER
0 - 1000mph	42 seconds
Length of track	10 miles
Current record	763 mph

3 ENGINES
Eurojet EJ200 (Eurofighter Typhoon)	90 kN
Hybrid Rocket	122 kN
Cosworth CA2010 (Formula 1 Engine)	**750 bhp**

The Cosworth CA2010 Formula 1 Engine is used to pump one tonne of (HTP) High Test Peroxide (H²O²) in 20 seconds. (42.6 litres per second)

COSWORTH CA2010 / CA2011 SPECIFICATION

DESIGNATION : CA2010 / CA2011
DUTY CYCLE TYPE : 4 stroke reciprocating piston, normally aspirated
CONFIGURATION : 8 cylinders in banked V configuration with an angle of 90 degrees
CONSTRUCTION : Cast aluminium alloy cylinder block and head, forged aluminium pistons, steel crankshaft
CAPACITY : 2,400cc
VALVES : 32 with pneumatic valve springs
MAXIMUM RPM : limited to 18,000rpm
TIMING : Double overhead cams driven via compliant gear from crankshaft
MASS : In excess of 95kg
POWER OUTPUT : In excess of 300bhp per litre
CYLINDER BORE : Less than 98mm
FUELLING : 8 injectors supplied by a pressurized system at 100bar
IGNITION : 8 ignition coils each driving single spark plug
LUBRICATION : Dry sump
SPARK PLUGS : Champion

Below are more incredible CA2010 / CA2011 facts.

Valves
The speed and precision of the engine valve movements (which allow air and fuel to enter and exhaust gases to exit the cylinder) are crucial to the power and performance of the CA2010 / CA2011. A pneumatic spring system is employed to enable the frequency to be achieved while maintaining absolute control over valve position. At maximum engine speed, each valve opens and closes 150 times per second. That's the same as a hummingbird's wing speed (the ruby-throated hummingbird).

Air Intake
At peak power the CA2010 / CA2011 ingests air fast enough to empty a typical living room in about 60 seconds, a task that would take over 20 minutes for the average home vacuum.
(We don't suggest you use a CA2010 / CA2011 to clean your carpets!)

Piston Speed
The speed of the piston is of course closely linked to overall engine speed. At maximum engine speed each piston will travel up and down the cylinder bore (a distance of 39.75mm) 300 times each second – that's 30 times in the blink of a human eye.

Crankshaft
The CA2010 / CA2011 crank shaft which transmits the engine power to the gearbox in the car, rotates up to 18,000 times each minute. During a typical race, at Monza for example, this crank shaft will spin approximately 22,000 times each lap and will have completed an amazing 1.17 million revolutions by the end of the 53 laps that make up race distance.

To meet the engine life restrictions that require each driver to use no more than 8 engines in the season, this same crank will then need to do the whole thing again at least twice more. This gives a lifetime total approaching 3.5 million revolutions in which the crankshaft transfers over 750 horsepower to the gearbox equivalent to 0.56 Mega Watts.

Connecting Rod Strength
At 18000 rpm the peak acceleration for each piston is 8600g (i.e. 8600 x force of gravity) – over 2000 times greater than the peak cornering and braking figures for an F1 car. This piston acceleration is equivalent to a weight of around 2.5 tons (or the weight of a Range Rover) pulling on the connecting rod.

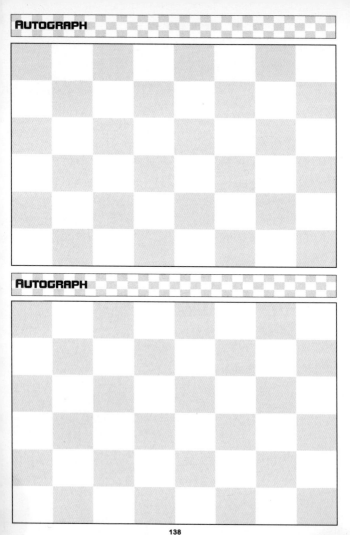

ChequeredFlagMedia

HTTP www.F1PocketBook.com or www.Motor-Racing.net

t www.twitter.com/RacingTorque or www.twitter.com/Racing_Torque

f www.facebook.com/pages/F1-Book/183856304979313

●● www.flickr.com/ChequeredFlag/sets

THANK YOU . . . .

We would like to take this opportunity to thank the following contributors, friends, colleagues & F1 Teams for their very kind help, assistance and patience.

Red Bull Racing
Vodafone McLaren Mercedes
Scuderia Ferrari Marlboro
Mercedes GP Petronas F1 Team
Lotus Renault GP
Williams F1
Force India F1 Team
Sauber F1 Team
Scuderia Toro Rosso
Team Lotus
Hispania Racing F1 Team
Marussia Virgin Racing

Pirelli & C. SpA
Cosworth - CA2010 / CA2011 Engine Details
Allianz SA - Circuit Images
Bloodhound SSC - Land Speed Record Attempt
FIA - Regulations & Research
Wikipedia - Research
StatsF1.com - Stats Comparison & Research
David Hayhoe - Grand Prix Data Book

Special Thanks To
James Allen - Foreword
Inprint Litho - Graphics & Printing (Lee & Damien)
Sophia & Danique
Cathy
Michaela

Do you know the average time it took for a F1 pit stop in the 1960s?

Prepare to laugh.....In the early 60's and late 50's it took about 3-4minutes. There were no pit stop garages, drivers pulled up on the side of the road, climbed out, along came the mechanics with their tools around their waists, lifted the bonnet and did some tuning, slowly replaced the tyres, driver climbed back in and drove off. There were about three mechanics in total. Today's average pit stop takes about 3-4 seconds, once stationary.